Office Politics
for the
Utterly Confused

Other books in the **Utterly Confused** Series include:

Job Hunting for the Utterly Confused
by Jason Rich

Financial Planning for the Utterly Confused,
Fifth Edition, by Joel Lerner

Office Politics for the Utterly Confused

Rosemary Salmon
William Salmon

McGraw-Hill

New York   San Francisco   Washington, D.C.   Auckland   Bogotá
Caracas   Lisbon   London   Madrid   Mexico City   Milan
Montreal   New Delhi   San Juan   Singapore
Sydney   Tokyo   Toronto

Library of Congress Cataloging-in-Publication Data

Salmon, Rosemary.
    Office politics for the utterly confused / Rosemary Salmon,
William Salmon.
        p.   cm.
    Includes bibliographical references and index.
    ISBN 0-07-058046-4
    1. Office politics.   I. Salmon, William A.   II. Title.
HF5386.5.S25   1999
650.1'3—dc21   98-44546
                                                             CIP

McGraw-Hill

A Division of The McGraw·Hill Companies

2   3   4   5   6   7   8   9   0   DOC/DOC   9   0   3   2   1   0   9

ISBN 0-07-058046-4

The sponsoring editor for this book was Betsy Brown, the editing liaison was
Patricia V. Amoroso, and the production supervisor was Clare B. Stanley.
It was set in Times Ten by North Market Street Graphics.

Printed and bound by R. R. Donnelley & Sons Company.

McGraw-Hill books are available at special quantity discounts to use as
premiums and sales promotions, or for use in corporate training programs.
For more information, please write to the Director of Special Sales, McGraw-
Hill, 11 West 19th Street, New York, NY 10011. Or contact your local bookstore.

This book is printed on recycled, acid-free paper containing a
minimum of 50% recycled de-inked fiber.

Contents

Preface

Office Politics for the Utterly Confused is intended to describe the variety of choices we all have in the way we work with others. This book focuses on the appropriate political skills we need to negotiate priorities, collaborate on complex assignments, and secure the necessary resources we need to complete important projects. Throughout this book, we advocate a positive approach to office politics and encourage practices that are built on credibility, trust, and mutual respect.

With a spirit of fair play as a guiding principle, we talked to dozens of professional associates and got permission from several of them to quote excerpts from our interviews with them. Two individuals were especially helpful along the way, and we acknowledge their enthusiastic support. Steve Ozer provided insights from an internal perspective about techniques that he knows individuals have used successfully to get ahead in his organization. Lonnie Barone provided ideas from an external perspective and focused on ways many of his corporate clients have developed and maintained credibility, an important component of positive political behavior. All of the colleagues and friends we interviewed added interesting insights and valuable data to our research, and we thank them for their contributions.

The most important challenge for us was to provide specific techniques to help individuals achieve exceptional results and maximum job satisfaction without manipulating, embarrassing, or hurting anyone else. We believe that it is possible to have extraordinary success at work each day and still sleep well at night. A clear conscience comes from practicing the ethical and responsible behaviors we outline in this book. We sincerely hope it helps.

Acknowledgments

- Excerpts from *The Empowered Manager* by Peter Block are reprinted with permission of Jossey-Bass Publishers, San Francisco, California. (See pages 1, 11, 13, 70, 82, 83, 119, 150, and 187.)

- Andrew Denka's comments about office politics appeared in *Personnel Journal,* October 1995, and are reprinted with permission of Workforce, ACC Communications, Inc., Costa Mesa, California. (See page 7.)

- Information about the Johari Window is based on P. C. Hanson's "The Johari Window: A Model for Soliciting and Giving Feedback" from *The 1973 Annual Handbook for Group Facilitators* and is reprinted with permission of Jossey-Bass Publishers, San Francisco, California. (See pages 92 to 96.)

- Information about the Thomas-Kilmann Conflict Model is adapted from the *Thomas-Kilmann Conflict Mode Instrument,* © Xiacom, Incorporated, Tuxedo, New York, and is reprinted with their permission. (See pages 130 and 133 to 136.)

- Excerpts from *Lighten Up* by C. W. Metcalf and Roma Felible are reprinted with permission of Addison Wesley Longman, Reading, Massachusetts. (See pages 172, 174, 182, and 183.)

- Excerpts from *Making Sense of Humor* by Lila Green are reprinted with permission of Knowledge, Ideas & Trends, Inc., Manchester, Connecticut. (See pages 169, 170, and 181.)

CHAPTER 1

Exploding the Myths About Office Politics

Man is by nature a political animal.—**Aristotle**

Politics is the pursuit of power, and power is both a function of position in the hierarchy, and, more importantly, a state of mind.—**Peter Block,** *The Empowered Manager* **(Jossey-Bass, 1988)**

Who is most likely to get ahead in today's chaotic and competitive business world? According to a March 1997 *Wall Street Journal* report, "bosses still tend to hire and promote people they're comfortable with—in other words, good politicians." In fact, "the degree to which politics, not performance, affects organizational decisions" was described as the most stress-producing aspect of business today in a recent survey of 1,880 executives conducted by Cornell University and Ray & Berndtson executive recruiting firm.

Mergers, reorganizations, downsizing, and other potentially disruptive activities have only made matters worse. Individuals and work groups now compete with each other more than ever for position, money, responsibility, and power. Success often depends on knowing how to get, use, and keep these important resources—

especially power. In fact, in a January 1997 *Fortune* article, Thomas A. Stewart warns that: "If you want to get ahead of the curve and stay there, you need to understand that power isn't what it was 20 years ago. You need to understand the sources and uses of power to thrive in business or to have a piece of it yourself."

In her article "How to Make Politics in Your Office Beneficial" (*The Plain Dealer,* February 26, 1995), Lisa M. Gunther observes that office politics, in its normally negative sense, can "poison the work environment and reduce us to simply enduring our jobs." However, Ms. Gunther endorses another side of office politics. "With some courage and creativity," she contends, "you can play office politics, retain your integrity and honesty, improve your work environment, and increase your job satisfaction. And, hang on, you can have fun, too." That side of office politics is the one we will emphasize in this book. It is the approach that may have gone out of style during the "Me Generation." It is the approach about which unprincipled office politicians do not have a clue, but it is the one that is being practiced today in organizations that value teamwork and quality service. Figure 1.1 illustrates some of the significant differences between positive and negative politics. We will concentrate on positive political techniques.

The notion of positive politics is also consistent with the original definition of the word. According to Webster's *New World Dictionary,* the word *politics* comes from the Greek *politikos* meaning "of a citizen." The word's primary meaning is having practical wisdom, being prudent, shrewd, diplomatic. Its secondary meaning is being crafty or unscrupulous. The word *politic* is also associated with Greek and Latin roots that gave us the words *police* ("the regulation within a state of morals, safety, and public order") and *polite* ("having or showing good culture, taste, and manners—especially being courteous, considerate, and tactful").

Therefore, the way you look at office politics will determine whether you resist or master this important aspect of organizational

Positive Politics	versus	Negative Politics
Straightforward		Manipulative
Win-Win		Win-Lose
Collaborative		Aggressive
Builds		Beats
Greater Good		Self-Interests
Panoramic View		Snapshot
Long-Term Strategy		Short-Term Measures
Empowering		Power-Hungry
Creates Credibility		Creates Resentment
Genuine		Artificial
Productive		Destructive
Honest and Fair		Contrived and False
Giver		Taker
Welcomes Recognition		Thrives on Flattery

Figure 1.1

life. Of course, your thinking will be influenced by your own past experiences, future needs, current fears, and personal beliefs. If you have been victimized in the past by dirty politics, you will no doubt hesitate to use skills you believe others might misunderstand. You may develop a negative perspective based on the unacceptable behavior of a few people.

You may also adapt specific defense mechanisms to protect yourself from the harmful effects of office politics as you have experienced them in the past. You may take comfort by perpetuating certain myths about office politics which can actually limit your sphere of influence and prevent you from dealing effectively with various work situations. It is important to examine and challenge these myths by taking a broader, more informed and more objective view of reality. The myths create a false sense of security and might discourage you from developing certain skills and practices that others have used fairly and successfully. Here are a few common myths.

Myth 1: There are no politics in my office or in our company.

Reality: Politics is a fact of organizational life. Acknowledge its existence and its impact on your work. Politics is the way we get things done at work—it is individuals and teams competing for resources, responsibility, power, position, and privileges. Because our success is defined by those things, getting them will determine whether or not we are doing a good job. The way to get money, resources, project approvals, and all of the other factors that define success is to become effective at office politics. That does not mean playing dirty. It means building relationships, being diplomatic, collaborating with others, being an effective team player in a modern work environment that is more complex, diverse, ambiguous, and dynamic than ever before. Sociologist Dr. Jan Yager emphasizes that: "The concept of the team player is much more important than it was before. If you can't do it, you just can't get ahead. It's the key factor people are looking for in terms of promoting someone. The only person who will get ahead is the one who works well with colleagues."

Myth 2: If you are a good employee, you don't need to worry about office politics. Your performance will speak for itself.

Reality: Your performance may speak for itself, but you need to make sure the right people are paying attention to it. In today's hectic and ever changing business world, you need to take greater responsibility than ever to make sure your manager and other key people in your organization are aware of your talents, accomplishments, and career interests. Managing your own development and advancement often takes vigilant attention and skillful communication.

Sometimes you are walking a fine line between promoting yourself (pointing out to key managers how your recent achievements qualify you for challenging new opportunities) and being a team player (where fitting in with coworkers is a more acceptable quality than standing out from the crowd). Humility is not an asset when you are seeking a promotion or making sure that your current performance is acknowledged or rewarded. However, if your supervisor is put off or threatened by your personal accomplishments or by assertive behavior describing or defending your work, you may need to tailor your message so that others see your past track record as a natural prelude to your future career aspirations.

Myth 3: If I play fair, others will play by the same rules and be fair to me.

Reality: Today, it is more likely than ever that others in your organization *will* play fairly and that you will not encounter some of the old back-stabbing, manipulative, or aggressive behaviors often associated in the past with office politics.

In a 1995 *Westchester County Business Journal* article, Michael O'Reilly, an area manager for the Dale Carnegie Institute, described a change in traditional office politics because there are fewer people doing it and just simply less time for it: "If you're not producing, what you say about other people doesn't make a difference. Those people are really becoming separate from the pack, and they stand out from other people sooner. There's less room for unpleasant people in the workplace."

While the old definition of office politics—the scheming and maneuvering for power and personal advantage that occurs within a given group—historically has had strong negative connotations, there is a new approach described by Dr. Yager: "Positive office politics or behavior is being honest, genuine, reliable—these are all traits that you get known for if you present yourself consistently in that way."

Those positive traits will also help you when you *do* encounter someone who is not playing fairly. You need to remain professional and diplomatic in the face of someone else's abusive or hostile behavior. As R. Don Steel points out in *Office Politics: The Woman's Guide to Beat the System and Gain Financial Success:*

> You're not going to advance unless you confront people who are talking behind your back, sabotaging your work or doing any other destructive reputation-bashing. You have to be able to confront the person, do it in private without name-calling or attacking, and do it in a calm, straightforward, logical manner. Dirty Harry never shouts.

Myth 4: I don't need to worry about campaigning for my own career interests. "Self-promoting" is egotistical and arrogant. If I want to get ahead, I can depend on others higher in the organization to recognize and reward my talent and contributions.

Reality: This myth is related to myth 2 above. While managers and others higher in your organization have some responsibility for your training, development, and advancement, the best they can do is share that responsibility with you. A good manager will acknowledge and reward your exceptional performance; a good manager will be your advocate or champion when your work warrants support or special recognition. But if your current manager is less effective than others or too busy with his or her own career concerns, you will need to take charge of your own career interests. In those cases, self-promotion is a necessary strategic approach that you must be willing and able to take for your own personal and professional well-being.

Ironically, what may appear on the surface as self-centered may, in fact, be beneficial to your company and to others in your work group. What is good for you may actually have value to others. Waiting for someone higher to take responsibility for your next move may place unfair demands on someone who has different priorities and pressures. Independent action may be more appropriate and more consistent with the behaviors described by Rosabeth Moss Kanter in *When Giants Learn to Dance:* "The new kind of business hero . . . must learn to operate without the might of the hierarchy behind them. The crutch of authority must be thrown away and replaced by their own ability to make relationships, use influence, and work with others to achieve results."

Myth 5: Politics is game playing. It is an undignified, self-serving waste of productive work time.

Reality: Some "political" people are so concerned about playing the game that their productivity actually suffers. They waste their time (and sometimes yours) in negative, harmful, and counterproductive activities. Their CYA (cover your anatomy) behaviors can drain your energy, damage your morale, and wear out your patience. Because you cannot get rid of office politics, it is important to minimize the impact of negative practices and maximize the value of a more positive approach.

In the October 1995 issue of *Personnel Journal,* Andrew Denka describes this fact of organizational life.

> Office politics are basic to the business world. If allowed to get out of hand, they can be negative. But dealt with properly, they enable work to be accomplished more smoothly. Employees who want to advance in their careers must learn to make use of the positive "diplomacy" aspects of office politics. While politics will always be a part of any business environment, one key to success is knowing how to navigate all of the aspects—the good, the bad, and the ugly.

In *Caught in the Middle: How to Survive and Thrive in Today's Management Squeeze,* Lynda McDermott emphasizes the critical importance of understanding the nature, scope, and characteristics of politics in your own work environment: "Not determining what the organizational politics are, and not strategizing ways to maneuver your way successfully through them, can be organizationally suicidal." And Jeffrey K. Pinto describes *appropriate politics* as being "politically sensitive to the concerns (real or imagined) of powerful stakeholder groups." In *Power and Politics in Project Management,* he highlights a short list of appropriate political tactics and behaviors like: "making alliances with powerful members of other stakeholder departments, networking, negotiating mutually acceptable solutions to seemingly insoluble problems, and recognizing that most organizational activities are predicated on the give-and-take of negotiation and compromise."

Myth 6: Men and women play politics the same.

Reality: Men and women do very few things exactly the same.

Historically, many men accepted the old boy climb to the top as a fact of life—and dirty politics as sometimes a necessary side effect of getting ahead. Women, for very long only the observers of this behavior in the workforce, entered this arena leery of the negative picture they saw.

The truth is that many people, especially women, think of office politics as dirty, sleazy, and unprofessional. But to get ahead, you must know how to play the game; you must know the rules; and you must be able to get sponsors, mentors, advocates, or champions.

In a perfect world, there would be no need for this book about office politics. People would be paid fairly for their actual job performance. People would be promoted because they had demonstrated the necessary competencies to perform more challenging work. People would not feel the need to compete with a coworker for the resources required to do their job effectively.

In such a world, there would be no glass ceilings limiting the upward movement of talented individuals regardless of their sex, race, or national origin. Individuals would collaborate with each other on important projects that helped their companies achieve a common goal and satisfy important customer needs. Instead of backbiting, there would be friendly internal competition, and team-work would be the rule rather than the exception. Those in authority would recognize, appreciate, and reward the efforts of anyone who tried to do a good job.

Because this utopia does not yet exist, this book was written to serve as a guide for people who are mystified by the political smarts necessary to maintain or advance their status in today's marketplace. Although we hear often of the dirty office politics of those who got where they are by stepping on the backs of others, there really is a fair way to play this game. If playing fair to get ahead is a new concept for you, read on.

The days of the martini lunches, when mingling with the brass (or schmoozing, as the baby boomers called it) was a middle rung on the ladder to the top, are gone. First of all, in this fast-paced, electronic-calendar business world, no one on their way up has time for hour-long lunches. Instead, today's smart people make work hours count. They seek challenges and ask for "stretch" assignments where they can contribute, learn, shine, and advance. They soak up what works and shake off what doesn't and get on with things rather than stew in bitter juices of defeat. They align themselves with principled senior players who recognize exceptional performance and have the power to reward it or at least to bring it to the attention of those who can.

They know that in the grand scheme of things, most of us are not brain surgeons or rocket scientists, and that a missed opportunity is not the electric chair but a minor step back on the path ahead. They can laugh at themselves and take life and its foibles with a bit of salt. They usually play as hard as they work (witness the mixed-age joggers and pickup basketball players in the parks).

The face on today's top executives is not the gray-flannel one you see in old fifties movies. Today's managers are sharp, bright people who have succeeded because they had a plan and followed it. They didn't climb to the top on the backs of their coworkers but on success stories. Most of them are willing to share these success stories, and the person on the way up would be wise to listen and learn.

Office Politics for the Utterly Confused will examine the positive and essential aspects of this topic. The book will provide practical techniques for gaining and sustaining power with dignity and mutual respect. It will begin with suggestions about the benefits of playing fair and end with cautions about the negative impact of dirty politics.

CHAPTER 2

Eight Ways to Make Office Politics Work for You

People in power who have achieved great things have been those who have given their word lightly, who have known how to trick men with their cunning, and who, in the end, have overcome those abiding by honest principles.—**Niccolo Machiavelli**, *The Prince*

In being political we walk the tightrope between advocating our own position and yet not increasing resistance against us by our actions. The path we take is a mixture of two forces: the individual choices we make in adapting to our environment and the nature of the norms and values of the organization we find ourselves imbedded in.—**Peter Block**, *The Empowered Manager*

When asked to talk about office politics, most of the people we interviewed for this book began by describing some negative experience they have had with unscrupulous, manipulative, backbiting managers or coworkers who have stepped all over others on their way up the corporate ladder. For most people, office politics brings back memories of some Machiavellian figure who lied, cheated, took credit for the ideas of others, blamed others for their shortcomings, and got ahead at someone else's expense or by holding others back. At best, this negative political style needs to be recognized and managed especially in any organization that values cooperation, teamwork, and healthy morale. At its worst, this political style can be unethical and extremely detrimental to the health and security of a company and all its employees.

In an environment where internal competition is encouraged, an aggressive type of political behavior can have disruptive and counterproductive consequences. Managers need to be careful not to support activities that foster turf wars, perpetuate interdepartmental friction, and put personal achievement above company success. Employees need to be comfortable confronting negative political practices knowing they have management support for a different political style—one that is based on diplomacy, good will, and mutual respect for individual achievement in the pursuit of common organizational goals.

This positive side of office politics depends on people's ability to align their own individual interests with each other and with the interests of the company. It is based on a firm belief that people are intrinsically good, that they want to work together toward a common goal, and that they do not want to succeed by taking advantage of someone else. It requires vigilant attention by both managers and employees to the dynamics within their work groups so that personal agendas do not become more important than company objectives.

Because many of us have worked in hierarchical companies with patriarchal standards and practices, we believe that certain negative political activities—manipulating people, withholding information, jockeying for position or favor, being seen with certain people at the right time—are the only choices we have. These are elements of what Peter Block calls playing the game (conventional corporate politics), which he challenges and calls an ineffective option in today's organizations.

> The problem is that getting better at maneuvering-type politics is not a very satisfying solution, even though it works. Why get better at a bad game? Our purpose is to create a good game. The good game involves acting as an entrepreneur for our unit and being political in the best sense of the word. Being political as an act of service, contribution, and creation.

There are eight specific techniques you can use to make office politics (the good game) work for you. Each of the following chapters will examine in greater detail how you can use these techniques to your best advantage. As you read the following brief chapter descriptions, use Fig. 2.1 to do a quick self-assessment of how you are doing now with these eight techniques.

Personal Assessment

As you read the brief chapter descriptions of the following techniques, evaluate how you are currently doing with office politics:

	Needs Work	Good	Exemplary
Technique #1: Build Alliances/Partnerships with the Right People	❏	❏	❏
Technique #2: Establish Collaborative Relationships with Peers	❏	❏	❏
Technique #3: Know & Contribute to Your Company's Objectives	❏	❏	❏
Technique #4: Tell the Truth	❏	❏	❏
Technique #5: Be Professional in the Way You Look and Act	❏	❏	❏
Technique #6: Choose Your Battles Strategically	❏	❏	❏
Technique #7: Take Charge of Your Morale & Your Career	❏	❏	❏
Technique #8: Maintain a Sense of Humor	❏	❏	❏

Figure 2.1

Technique 1: Build Alliances/Partnerships with the Right People

Your success often depends on your ability to be perceived as one of your company's most valuable assets. Obviously, doing excellent work is the first requirement. Then, making sure other important people know about your accomplishments and talk about them to each other will require skillful attention and political savvy. John Goodard once said, "If you really know what things you want out of life, it's amazing how opportunities will come to enable you to carry them out."

Chapter 3 presents ways to help you gain and maintain the respect of managers and others who have formal power in your organization. We will help you identify those key players who have informal power because of length of service, special knowledge or expertise, strategic positions, or association with key customers. Specific action steps will be reviewed for making and strengthening connections with these important individuals and ways will be suggested to get their attention through your exceptional performance on the job.

Technique 2: Establish Collaborative Relationships with Peers

Your success often depends on your ability to influence or persuade others to cooperate with you. There are many personal qualities (like honesty and dependability) that can help you build effective relationships. There are also many interpersonal skills (like active listening and shared decision making) that can let others know you value their ideas and respect them as individuals.

Chapter 4 describes ways to build networks that are mutually beneficial. You will be encouraged to identify key constituents, customers, and coworkers so that you have a current list of people you need to work with effectively. We will analyze what makes an effective team and recommend specific competencies that will help make you a valued team player.

Technique 3: Know Your Company's Strategic Objectives

Your value to your organization will depend on the contribution you are making to its success. As Henry David Thoreau once observed, "It's not enough to be busy. The question is: What are we busy about?" One of the simplest summaries of the Total Quality Management (TQM) movement that has swept through the business world in the past 20 years is "do the right thing right the first time."

We recommend in this chapter that you pay close attention to your effectiveness—(choosing the right goals and getting results) and efficiency (choosing the best way to accomplish your company's most important priorities). We encourage you to make certain that you contribute to current goals, initiatives, and opportunities. You will discover ideas to help you stay informed about industry trends and new business possibilities. We encourage you to keep your personal goals in line with those of your organization so that your career success is a natural by-product of your job success. It is recommended that you be visible and vocal in your support of relevant corporate activities and that you make sure that key managers know your worth and what it would cost the company if you left.

Technique 4: Tell the Truth

Your success depends on your willingness to take responsibility for your actions and ownership of your reactions to other people and situations. Looking for alibis, excuses, or scapegoats can give others the impression that you are not willing to face the facts, tell the truth, or confront problems honestly and directly. One of the rules of success that General Electric's CEO, Jack Welch, talks about is: "Face reality as it is—not as it was, and not as you wish it were. Be candid, up-front, and totally honest with everyone."

This chapter emphasizes that you build a foundation of credibility and trust by making sure that others know they can depend on you to tell the truth and come through for them. Ways are suggested to help you keep your promises and follow through on your commitments. We will review basic communication skills, especially listening skills, so that you can operate with all the data you need to make informed, intelligent decisions.

Technique 5: Be Professional in the Way You Look and Act

Your success often depends on unwritten rules about business etiquette and workplace courtesy. Personal appearance will always be an important part of your company's professional standards. Certain social skills are obvious (like using mouthwash and deodorant so that you are not offensive to others). Other social situations are less obvious and may need to be discussed (like defining what your company means by casual clothing so that your choices are not too provocative, distracting, or relaxed).

Chapter 7 considers some of the current ways organizations and individuals define the word *professionalism*. We will reinforce many of the obvious rules of polite interactions with others—punctuality, maintaining confidentiality, returning messages in a timely way, and respecting other people's time, property, and physical space.

We will also advocate not being a party to back-stabbing, name-calling, finger-pointing, or other underhanded practices. You will be encouraged to avoid the rumor mill, and we suggest ways for you to be a leader, not a follower. Discover specific things you can practice to develop social savvy about what you can do or say in the presence of coworkers. We will suggest ways to deal with changing dress-for-success policies. Ideas for learning about and adapting to your company's culture and the way "things are done around here" should help you to adjust.

Technique 6: Choose Your Battles Strategically

Your professional success depends on your ability to recognize the most significant obstacles to your own performance. Some situations or events will be minor inconveniences, temporary setbacks that require only minimal attention. Other problems will require immediate and sustained concentration because they can have a potentially damaging effect on your work and your reputation. Certain interactions with people around you can lead to disagreements and an uncomfortable tension that must be resolved.

We encourage you to be assertive when you need to be and not to sweat the small stuff. A series of strategies and action steps is presented to help you deal with interpersonal conflicts quickly and effectively. We recommend that you confront people and issues that are having a negative impact on *your* performance and provide action steps for you to use when dealing with difficult people or situations.

Technique 7: Take Charge of Your Own Morale and Your Own Career

Your success in life is up to you. It is your own business! And that may be one of the best ways for you to think about the work you are doing. Imagine that you are self-employed and that your professional success depends largely on your ability to produce outstanding results today and to make informed decisions about your future. In fact, you will be more productive in your current job if you take ownership and accountability for what is happening to you at work. Christopher Morley once said, "There is only one success—to be able to spend your life in your own way."

You will learn suggestions to help you avoid falling into the trap of depending on others to manage your work, your development, and your career. We will recommend various resources to enhance your current competencies and job skills. Also, we will demonstrate how maintaining a positive attitude, outlook, and approach to your job can be the best way to advance your career and get challenging new assignments.

Technique 8: Maintain a Sense of Humor

Your success depends on your ability to keep things in perspective. Ethel Barrymore once said, "You grow up the day you have your first real laugh at yourself." There are no real advantages to taking yourself or your work too seriously. Having a sense of humor can help provide a balanced view of life and can help you give appropriate attention to those things that are worrying you. Taking things in stride will help you keep pace with others. A good sense of humor creates positive energy and prevents negative feelings from slowing you down or holding you back.

This chapter discusses tactics that can help you keep things in perspective. We encourage you to be cordial, diplomatic, and cheerful even in difficult situations. The best way to gain power is by gaining the respect of others. We will demonstrate that a good sense of humor is often the best way to help you maintain balance, perspective, and a spirit of cooperation. We caution you, however, about inappropriate attempts at humor that offend and embarrass others.

Our experience consulting with managers, supervisors, and employees of both small companies and large Fortune 500 corporations has given us a feel for the broad range of experiences people have in the workplace. We were particularly interested in, and subsequently interviewed, individuals who have succeeded in their jobs by using ethical and commonsense methods for advancement. Because many of their work experiences are common to all of us, some of their stories and comments may help you tailor your own approaches and clarify your own future career choices.

To ensure that our view reflects what others are experiencing, we interviewed more than 25 people in various job positions in a wide cross section of the business world. A dozen of these individuals agreed to let us quote them by name when describing some of their personal experiences with office politics. One of the people we wanted to interview agreed to meet with us by saying, "I would be happy to tell you what I think. Actually, office politics means that you go to the office parties, go to the office picnics, drink the Kool-Aid, and do what you're told." This cynical reference to the Jim Jones cult mass suicide in Guyana almost 20 years ago raised obvious concerns for us. We decided not to schedule an interview with that person because he was having a difficult time managing his own morale, a key technique for making office politics work today.

Another potential interviewee described his experiences as: "Tell management what they want to hear even if it means compromising your own principles. Honesty is not always the best policy, especially when you work for hatchet men who enjoy killing messengers." Again, we found this perception to be the exception rather than the rule, so we opted to shorten the interview and thanked the person for what we truthfully discovered was as a minority opinion.

Overall, we collected valuable information from these interviews, and we thank everyone who helped us sharpen our point of view and expand our frame of reference. We have organized this material in a format that we hope will be useful to you. Chapters 3 through 12 each include:

- Questions at the beginning that will help you decide quickly whether you need or want to read this information
- Quick advice on the most important points of each subject from experts in the field
- Practical step-by-step actions for each technique
- Easy reminders of essential aspects of each topic
- Red alerts about common problems and dangers that arise in many political situations
- Practical shortcuts and quick tips
- Chapter summaries and reviews

We conclude the book with some warnings about the negative impact of dirty politics and highlight, in closing, the benefits of fair play. We hope that this information and approach is user-friendly to you now and a handy reference resource to you in your future work pursuits.

CHAPTER 3

◆◆◆◆◆◆◆◆◆◆◆◆◆◆◆◆◆◆◆◆◆◆◆◆◆◆◆◆

POLITICAL TECHNIQUE 1

Build Alliances/ Partnerships with the Right People

◆◆◆◆◆◆◆◆◆◆◆◆◆◆◆◆◆◆◆◆◆◆◆◆◆◆◆◆

You seldom accomplish very much by yourself. You must get the assistance of others.—**Henry J. Kaiser**

Overall, the power of the position is giving way to the power of the person. A formal title and its placement on an organization chart have less to do with career prospects and career success . . . than the skills and ideas a person brings to that work.—**Rosabeth Moss Kanter,** *When Giants Learn to Dance*

Do I Need to Read This Chapter?

→ Who are the people who have formal or informal power to influence your work and your career?

→ How do you determine who the right people are, and how do you develop effective relationships with them?

→ How do you determine who the wrong people are, and how do you avoid being associated with them?

◆◆◆

Power is the ability to influence others to act or respond in a particular way, to get things done the way the person with power wants them done. For many of us, the word *power* has a negative connotation, one that we associate with the misuse or abuse of power in a manipulative, egotistical, or underhanded way. We have all known bullies; we have all read about tyrants and dictators; we can all name people who have exploited others and used their authority to intimidate, coerce, or control. We talk about power plays—those situations in which certain people have flexed their muscles and overpowered others with their words, their organizational connections, or their threats of retaliation. Many of us are so uncomfortable with these negative examples of aggressive power that we have a difficult time seeing power as the basis for viable, positive political action within our organization.

However, most of us have some degree of power that comes to us from several possible sources as listed.

- Position we hold in the company
- Our personal qualities, talents, and experiences
- Information we can access
- Resources we control
- Relationships we have developed with others

As you read the following brief descriptions about the nature and source of power in your organization, use Fig. 3.1 to do a quick assessment of how much power you currently have and why.

Position power is based on any legitimate authority associated with our jobs. For example, managers influence others because they have the legitimate authority to enforce company policies and because they have control of organizational rewards like pay increases, promotions, challenging work assignments, and other forms of recognition. Similarly, a safety expert may have the legitimate authority to stop a questionable production process; an executive secretary may have the power to schedule or cancel meetings

TYPE OF POWER	AMOUNT OF POWER YOU HAVE (LOW-MEDIUM-HIGH)	SOURCE OF YOUR POWER
Position Power		
Personal Power		
Information Power		
Resource Power		
Relationship Power		
Other Power or Influence		

Figure 3.1

for a boss; an accountant may have the authority to question a costly construction project; a corporate lawyer may have the power to stop an illegal hiring practice. All of these are examples of position power, and all of us usually have some degree of legitimate authority associated with our jobs.

Personal power comes from those qualities, traits, or practices that allow us to influence the behavior of others. Sometimes this type of power is based on a specific expertise or special knowledge. Computer specialists have personal power when they are discussing the latest technology. Marketing specialists have personal power when they are explaining demographic trends. Sometimes this type of power comes from personal qualities that we usually describe with admiring words like charisma, charm, integrity, or credibility. People with this type of personal power are able to influence us because we like them, trust them, or believe in them. We'll follow their example, go along with them, or accept what they recommend because we really have no reason to resist. That makes them irresistible in a positive sense of the word.

Information power comes from the ability to help others deal with confusion or uncertainty. For example, the first group to learn how to use a new computer program has information power that can be useful to other users when it is their turn to learn the new system. Likewise, individuals involved in pilot programs or test processes have an advantage that gives them information power with others who have not been introduced to these new methodologies. Veteran employees know more about the company's unwritten rules than new employees do, and members of special project teams often know the course of action their company intends to take long before the rest of the employees.

In *Powershift* (Bantam Books, 1990), Alvin Toffler describes how information affects organizational power.

> Virtually every "fact" used in business, political life, and everyday human relations is derived from other "facts" or assumptions that have been shaped, deliberately or not, by the preexisting power structure. Every "fact" thus has a power-history and what might be called a power future—an impact, large or small, on the future distribution of power.

People in the know often make choices about how they use information to improve relationships or isolate themselves from others who can benefit from what they know.

Resource power comes from our ability to access or control resources, especially time, money, and people. The scarcer the resource, the more power we have. The amount of financial signing authority a person has is often a good indicator of resource power. If I need to get my supervisor's authorization to buy a $50 tool, I have less resource power than someone who can select and purchase a new computer without needing to ask for approval. The person who determines the budget and establishes spending restrictions usually has more power than the person who actually spends the money. The person who sponsors a project team or authorizes certain individuals to participate and give their time to the effort usually has more resource power than the project team leader or the team members.

Relationship power is based on the individual contacts we have made and maintained. The more connections we have with the right people, the stronger our base of power. If we have developed a network of peers, customers, managers, suppliers, and key employees at all levels of our organization, then we have enhanced our relationship power. The challenge is determining who the *right* people are, how much time we can afford to dedicate to our networking activities, and what we are able to bring to these relationships that will be useful to the other person. Time is such a precious resource when we are at work that we need to be both honest and selective about our networking activities. Two questions can help: "How can this person I am making or keeping contact with help me be more productive, effective, or efficient?" and "What information, resource, support, or help can I reciprocate with that will make this relationship beneficial to the other person?"

One person we interviewed spoke of the importance of aligning yourself with the right people.

There are those people who are not in positions of authority today, but you know they are being groomed, they have a good reputation, and you know they are on the way up. Helping them out on their way up can help you in the long run. Help them solve a problem, resolve an issue, anything that will make life easier for them—they will remember. For example, I had a call a few years ago, a special request for help from the manager of one of our key business units. The easiest thing for me was to say "that's not my job." But I did the work on my own time, and a few months later that individual came back to my boss and requested me again for another project. Before long, I was working full-time in that other business area. It was a nice promotion for me.

Quick Tips

Q: Who has formal power in your organization today?

A: Use Fig. 3.2 to make a short list of the five or six most influential people in your part of the organization. The list should include your immediate supervisor and his or her manager. Include people on your list who have the power to affect your work. Remember that they may work in other departments or locations.

Q: How has the current organization chart changed in the past few years?

A: Compare organization charts from recent years to help you determine who has gotten promoted, transferred, or ignored. Note which departments have grown, shrunk, or disappeared. Use Fig. 3.2 to list any rising stars you may want to add to your earlier list of powerful people.

Q: Who has informal power in your organization?

A: Use Fig. 3.2 to identify people with informal authority or influence, and try to determine the source of their power. Did they get it because of length of service, special knowledge or expertise, strategic position, association with key customers, or some other special contribution? Ask yourself whether these people with informal power know you and the quality of your work. Ask yourself also how you can become more visible and credible with these key people.

A person who is secure in his or her position may not be threatened by your questions about what is really going on in your company. You may be able to get specific information about:

- Who really has power or influence with senior management?

- What kind of projects are getting management's attention and support?

- Which individuals are on their way up in the organization and which individuals have peaked or lost favor?

Once you have identified the people around you who have both formal and informal power, consider ways that are available for you

YOUR "IN" BOX OF INFLUENTIAL PEOPLE

Individuals with Formal Power: **Rising Stars:**

1. _____   1. _____

2. _____   2. _____

3. _____   3. _____

4. _____   4. _____

5. _____   5. _____

6. _____   6. _____

Individuals with Informal Power: **What Is the Source of Their Influence?**

1. _____   _____

2. _____   _____

3. _____   _____

4. _____   _____

5. _____   _____

6. _____   _____

Figure 3.2

to meet and work with them. For example, you might want to think about informal lunch meetings, project teams, sending copies of your reports to these key people, or asking for their advice on an important assignment.

Individuals can exert influence in a variety of ways. Managers, for example, can give orders to their direct reports, or they can encourage participation in essential decision-making activities. They can limit creativity and accountability, or they can empower people to take an active role solving problems or addressing performance issues. Coworkers can also influence each other by offering suggestions, providing timely service, collaborating on difficult problems, and working together to meet the needs of important customers. Of course, the opposite can also occur, and peers can let power plays, conflicting priorities, or old-fashioned turf wars stand in the way of teamwork and cooperation.

Sometimes building collaborative relationships with superiors takes ingenuity and a willingness to take risks. Johanna Zitto, president of JZ Consulting & Training, Inc., remembers how she handled a difficult situation in a difficult environment.

I worked in a Fortune 300 office system corporation. It was a highly competitive work environment. I tried to establish collaborative relationships, but for many, it was a back-stabbing, cutthroat division. Once, I did a lot of work on a special project and wrote a final report that our team planned to send to corporate headquarters. I gave my boss a "courtesy copy." He told my assistant to take my name off the report and put his name on it instead. Because of my relationship with my assistant, Margie, she told me. I went in to talk to my boss. Since I had to maintain a constructive relationship with him, I had to deal with him in a way that didn't make him seem like a scoundrel. I knew if I confronted him about taking credit for my ideas or put Margie in the middle that he would look for ways to get even, probably with both of us. So I faxed the report to headquarters with my name on it, and just asked him what he thought of the report I had faxed up to corporate. He got the message, and I learned a lesson. From then on, I survived in that company by helping people like Margie get what they wanted so they would help me get what I needed to succeed.

Katherine Huston, currently senior vice president for the Gabriel Group, describes an uncomfortable situation she had to deal with when she reported to a boss who was not respected by his peers.

If your boss is "out" politically and is not well-regarded, it is very difficult for you. I suffered sometimes because I had a boss who was not well thought of, and I got tainted by that. Dealing with that is a difficult tightrope walk. You want to be well-regarded, so you do your best work and let it be known afterward that you were an important part of getting the job done effectively. It's important for you never to talk about your boss in the same negative way that others are doing, and it keeps you free in both regards—with your boss and with other key individuals. At times, you may want to say something to your boss about how he is being viewed by others, but you have to do that very gingerly, very carefully because you run the risk of being seen as part of the problem.

Danger!

- Build alliances with several key people so that if any one person leaves or loses favor, your reputation and credibility will not be seriously damaged.

Individuals can also exert upward influence by filtering data they pass on to their managers or by withholding information they perceive to be detrimental to their jobs or their careers. Employees can also punish their supervisors by limiting the quantity or quality of their work, and they can reward their supervisors by meeting or exceeding performance expectations.

Your personal and professional success depends on other people. You can only go so far alone; you simply cannot succeed in life without help from others. If you want to achieve all you are capable of, you must have support from others, you must have the right people behind you and on your side. One of the best ways for you to be successful is to build alliances or partnerships with the right people—those key individuals who can help you the most and who depend on you for their success.

Joseph Toto, director of Organizational Effectiveness for Hoffmann-LaRoche, Inc., highlights the importance of building partnerships.

People need to take the time to build relationships. There are many long-term benefits, and we need to recognize the importance of these alliances. Most are based on the nature of the work people do with each other. Sometimes, you are privy to sensitive, vulnerable data. You become exposed to critical information, and the way you handle it will cement your ability to be trustworthy and trusted in the future. If you violate that trust, the person will know it, and your behavior will damage your long-term relationship. If you want to build future alliances, you need to take the time to know the other person, to understand the other person's needs, concerns, and interests. You do this by asking and listening and making a respectful response that lets them know they are being heard. One of the best ways to build rapport with the right people is to communicate effectively with their support staff or other managers and professionals who work for them. My advice to people trying to build relationships is simply: Don't remain a stranger—let others know who you are, why you are there, and how you can help them.

For LaSalle University professor Marianne Gauss, building alliances has been an interesting learning process.

Some of it has been serendipity, some of it has been conscious and intentional. When I graduated from LaSalle, I was put on the alumni board. At first there was some frustration because the other members were all men. I was in the second class of women ever elected to the board. The men would talk about basketball all the time. I felt like quitting, but said to myself, "You can't change things from the outside." I eventually became the first woman ever to be board president. My association with that group helped me when I went to work at the university. There was a sense on campus that I had influence, that I was someone to know, that I had linkages to a powerful group. I also had a strong advocate, the provost. He wouldn't break policy, but he did support me and let others know he was one of my sponsors. The most important thing is to do your job, do what you are being paid to do. My power with the board grew out of a genuine affection for the people I was working with, not out of an interest to build a base of power. Today, I try to have lunch with people in other departments because I like them, enjoy their company, and want to spend time with them. When speaking to students, I recommend that they treat people politely, be social, available, kind. I try to encourage them to save energy for the battles that count, maintain a sense of humor, and think outside the box.

For Steve Ozer, a communications manager for the Rohm and Haas Company, the real challenge with building relationships is often a question of time management.

There are more requests for your time than you can possibly handle. So you have to prioritize and decide whose request to table, delegate, or send to someone else. The challenge is determining: "Who are the people you need to deliver for and why?" You can't satisfy everyone, so you need to decide which tasks will add the greatest value to your organization. You can't say *yes* to everyone, so you need to make sure you're not diminishing your own value by trying to do too much and damaging your own reputation by doing work that is below your own quality standards. One of the worst political mistakes you can make is saying yes to everyone. You need to observe people—notice the results of what they do—and ask if they are making significant contributions to the results of the company.

Don't Forget

- Where you came from and who helped you get this far along.
- You don't move up the ladder by stepping on other people. Work hard to have your success cheered (not jeered) by others.
- Be willing to ask for help from people who will be flattered that you did.

Formal power is given to a person by virtue of his or her position in the company. An individual's job description or a specific box on the organizational chart can usually tell us how much formal power has been entrusted to that person. A first-line supervisor has more formal power than the employees who report to him or her, but less than the manager who is higher up the chain of command. This power of position is different from informal power which is earned by building relationships, demonstrating competence, sharing expertise, and having a positive impact on the work environment. To expand your informal power:

- Develop trusting relationships with others in your organization and in your industry. Start with your own work group, the people you deal with every day. Don't overlook the obvious and ignore those relationships that are probably most important to your immediate success. Then develop positive relationships with people in other areas of your company who affect (or are affected by) your work. These internal networks should include anyone who helps you determine your priorities or meet your perfor-

Get Started

1. Do a really good job. Let your performance speak for itself.

2. Expand your sphere of influence by volunteering for assignments you know you can do well. Build on previous successes.

3. Let key people know you are available for new opportunities.

4. Increase your visibility by attending professional meetings, company functions, and community activities sponsored by your organization.

5. Depending on the scope of your job, routinely visit key customers or other internal departments where partnerships and collaboration will contribute to your company's success.

6. Be upbeat and enthusiastic about your company's objectives and strategies. Be willing to offer suggestions without sounding negative, arrogant, or overly aggressive.

7. Let people know you appreciate them, their hard work, and any help they give you. Saying thanks is one of the simplest ways to build strong relationships.

mance objectives. Finally, build external networks by participating in professional associations that will help you stay current about industry trends and opportunities.

- Contribute to your company's success by meeting key objectives in a quality way on time and within budget. Keep those three measurement criteria (quality, time, and cost) in mind with everything you do. They are the most common standards organizations use to define success. Measuring your own performance and contribution that way should make an appropriate impression on your manager and other company executives.

- Be professional in the way you look and act. Demonstrate self-confidence and an air of competence in the way you approach your work.

When you are making a conscious effort to expand your informal power, the first challenge is to identify those people at work who can help you meet your goals, deliver the required results, and establish your reputation as an asset to the company. This will help you focus your available time and energies on the most important relationships.

Start by gaining and maintaining the respect of your managers and others who have formal power in your organization. The current organizational chart is a good way to identify individuals who have been given authority by others higher in the company. By comparing the latest chart with one from last year and one from a few years ago, you can also get a quick snapshot of key people on their way up the organizational pyramid as well as an idea of those who have plateaued, stalled, or gone backward.

Start by making your boss look good. Find out your immediate supervisor's major priorities or concerns and do your best to make a significant contribution to your team's efforts. If you are not sure about his or her expectations, ask questions and pay attention to the things that really matter. Here are a few common problems that could have important political implications for you:

- You are running behind schedule on an important project mostly because you are not getting the information or support you need from another department. You have tried talking to the people you deal with on a regular basis, but the problem has not been resolved. How soon would your boss like to know about this problem? What would your boss expect you to do next?

- There have been several unexpected expenses on one of your current assignments, and you are concerned about the budget constraints you discussed with your boss at the beginning of the project. Do you have the authority to go over budget to ensure a timely and effective outcome? Do you need your supervisor's permission to change specifications, get additional resources, or rearrange priorities?

- One of your key customers or constituents has asked you for special considerations on a critical project. In some ways, you see this request as compromising on the quality your team typically delivers, cutting corners to expedite delivery of a product to one of their important customers. What would your supervisor expect you to do in this situation? How involved would your boss want or need to be in your decision about this problem?

- You are spending an alarming amount of time at work trying to stay ahead of a surprising volume of new business. At first, you thought the changing demands were part of a temporary crunch, but it has been months now since you have been able to leave work on time. You have taken work home with you almost every night, and you have worked several weekends to try to catch up on your backlog. You are concerned because you do not see an end in sight. Your typically good performance is beginning to slip. Your boss is also exceptionally busy right now, but your workload has reached a crisis proportion. What would your supervisor expect you to do? How can you resolve this problem satisfactorily for both you and your boss?

Answers to questions like these will help you understand what is important to your supervisor and how you can meet his or her expectations. It is important for you to know what results your boss wants you to accomplish; it is critical for you to know how your boss wants you to accomplish those results and how your boss wants you to deal with problems, obstacles, or concerns. Your work relationship with your immediate supervisor is one of the most politically significant aspects of your job, and it requires serious and consistent attention. Get to know who your supervisor trusts and admires. Get to know your supervisor's likes and dislikes, advocates and enemies, accomplishments and challenges, wishes and worries. The more you know, the better and easier it will be for you to meet or exceed your supervisor's expectations.

Danger!

- Don't talk about others behind their backs. If you have a problem with someone, talk to him or her and get it resolved.

Katherine Huston believes that when you go into an environment, you really have to understand more than just your own specific area:

> It's really important to know the business, the people in it, and how you connect with them. For example, when I was at SmithKline, there was a manager in human resources who was very knowledgeable, and she became a mentor to me. The boss I had at the time was really not able to do that in the same way. My manager saw me as someone to be supervised, not as a human resource. So with him, there was a control-command aspect and my response to it, versus looking at me as a real partner and ally. The senior human resource manager and mentor saw me differently. She once described me, at that point in my career, as an unpolished gem. She saw my potential, and we quickly developed a symbiotic relationship. I learned a lot from her, and I helped her learn some things about our department's functions as well. She prepared me to write objectives for my area, whereas my boss assumed I should know the MBO [management by

objective] process and simply said, "Have your objectives developed and documented by the end of the week."

Another mentor helped me to see new opportunities and grow in the training area. He once said to me, "You're an administrator, and you do a very fine job. But the *real* value is in doing the training, and here's some of the specific ways you can be very powerful doing it." Another mentor once said, "You really need to know about the politics around here." When I said, "I don't want to be involved with the politics, I want to stay outside the fray," he responded: "If you know you're going into a jungle and you know there are snakes and snake pits in there, wouldn't you rather know where they are?" When I said, "Of course," he told me, "I can help you, then, know where they are so that you can move through the jungle relatively safely. And that's the reason you need to know about politics and what's going on." It was good advice, and I learned how important information like that can be.

My mentors told me, "You learn quickly, you soak up things like a sponge, and you are open." I was doing a good job in my current position, and I think these mentors saw that I had both the interest and the potential to do more. The benefit of alliances, partnerships, and networks is that, if you want to, you can grow and develop new competencies and do so in alignment with a business culture that values you and your abilities because they are targeted and consistent with the company's objectives.

Consider others in your department or proximate work area who also seem to be favored by senior management. Include on this list anyone who has had several promotions in the past few years, anyone who had been picked to lead special project teams (especially if they were successful), and anyone who gets invited to regular strategic or operational planning meetings. Think next about those individuals who have access to key decision makers, have any impact on budgeting or financial matters, and are involved in important company or departmental communication.

Susan McKeone, an internal consultant for a Fortune 500 specialty chemical company, believes building relationships with powerful people takes special skills.

I've had some painful lessons that have taught me that if you're doing work with influential people, you need to be cognizant of how others perceive your association. You need to be careful what you say about your relationships because others may see it as name-dropping. People may see what you're doing as a negative, and you may be perceived as a person with more power than you actually have. Sometimes you need to walk a fine line—earning the respect of those above you without damaging your credibility with your peers.

Shortcut

- Volunteer for special projects and teams that will give you a chance to demonstrate your talents and skills quickly to the right people.

Remember those coworkers or peers who have informal power because of length of service, special knowledge or expertise, strategic positions, or associations with key customers. Sometimes your rapport with an administrative assistant will determine whether you can schedule the meeting you need with his or her boss. Getting along well with one of your company's 20-year veterans can help you gain valuable practical information about how things *really* get done around here. And knowing someone who can give you the right technical answer the minute your computer takes an unexpected break can help you stay on line and on time with your important deadlines. The names of these key people will not jump out at you from any organizational chart. These are the individuals you get to know because you work with them every day or because your paths cross at critical times, on important projects, or when either one of you needs help. Which brings us to another important point: building alliances is a two-way street. The best partnerships are mutually beneficial. Both parties involved gain something from establishing and cultivating the relationship.

Once you have identified the right people you want to devote your time and energy to at work, the next step is to determine the best way to approach these individuals. Part of the key here is to remember that they are *individuals*, each with different needs, priorities, pressures, and preferences. Understanding and respecting their individuality will help you establish the right foundation for a successful work relationship. Ask yourself, "What do they need or want from me? What are they willing or able to give me to help me with my work? What is the best way for us to work together now so that our future dealings will be positive and productive?"

These questions can provide you with important insights about what motivates another person and what it will take to build a successful relationship with that individual. Obviously listening to what other people have to say—*really* paying attention so that you understand clearly and accurately what is important to them—will provide you with valuable information to help you develop the best kind of relationships. Observation is another way of gaining clues or cues about someone else's preferences and priorities. Taken together, the knowledge you accumulate about each key individual can help you tailor your approach and ensure success.

For example, if you work with someone who is analytical and detail-oriented, giving him or her timely and precise updates on a routine basis may be the best way to let him or her know that you recognize and respect his or her needs. That employee may also be the best person for you to call when you need facts, figures, or other historical evidence to support one of your proposed projects. On the other hand, if you work with someone who is more spontaneous and creative, you might find mutual benefit helping each other brainstorm about new approaches to persistent problems. Finally, there are several practices that work for most people—complimenting them for good work, thanking them for helping you on a tough project, sharing important information with them before being asked, asking for their help in areas where they have experience, expertise, or interest—actions that go a long way to building and maintaining teamwork and cooperation.

PARTNERSHIP AGREEMENT

In order for me to accomplish the following work objective, _____

_____

It will be important for me to establish or strengthen my working relationship with

_____

The benefit to me will be: _____

_____

The benefit to the other person will be: _____

_____

The benefit to others in the company will be: _____

_____

I would describe our current working relationship as _____.

To establish, maintain, or improve the way I work with this individual, I will have to:

_____

I think this effort is definitely worth the time, the energy, and the cost it will take

because _____.

Figure 3.3

Rosemary Adiletto, prevention program coordinator for Today, Inc. (a private, nonprofit drug and alcohol treatment organization), remembers how she overcame some initial obstacles to her eventual success.

Shortcut

- Use the Partnership Agreement form in Fig. 3.3 to help you focus your attention on the key aspects of any partnership you are planning to build. Notice that the emphasis is on accomplishing one of your key objectives.

When I felt I wasn't being accepted, I asked for help in understanding the operations. I asked them if I could observe them at their jobs. Then I wrote a memo to the executive director thanking him for the experience, and telling him how proud I was to be associated with the organization. To be successful, do a good job and be willing to change. Learn who the key players are, learn what their rules are, and make any ideas you have seem like their ideas.

Carol Tunstall, a human resource manager for a large chemical company, recommends that people concentrate on the job they are doing.

Don't be overly concerned with getting ahead. Build credibility with what you're doing now. It's important to do a good job and build an area of expertise. Then make sure people know what you've done. There's a fine line between bragging and modest self-promotion, but you can't always depend on others to recognize your accomplishments.

Once you have established a base of expertise, experience, and credentials, volunteer for lots of things. When opportunities come up, jump in and seize them, especially if you have the background to at least get started on the right foot. Look for opportunities to be a leader and to sell your ideas. Build credibility both with your technical expertise and your ability to work with people.

The best way to build relationships that will be most beneficial to you is to focus on the other person. Show that you are genuinely interested in them—what they are doing, why it is important, how you can help. Be a good listener. Pay close attention to what they are saying, both verbally and nonverbally. Ask good clarifying and probing questions to make sure you understand. Encourage people to talk about themselves. Make them feel important and do it sincerely! You will build a strong basis for future conversations. Remember, you are primarily interested in discovering what this person can do for you. The best way to find out is to learn as much as possible about him or her. Concentrate on your goal (getting information, support, resources that can help you) rather than on whether or not you like the other person. Focus on your performance and results and leave personalities out of the conversation as much as possible.

Gain a reputation for being competent and dependable. Pitch in and go the extra mile in front of the right people. Let your boss and other managers know that you are willing to go beyond your normal work routine and are able to stretch your skill base when something out of the ordinary is required. A friend once volunteered to edit and revise a report that a senior manager considered too wordy. It took time, effort, and concentration for this individual to condense a 35-page project team document into a clear, easy-to-read 15-page report that managers quickly held up as a model for future project summaries. The individual developed a reputation both as an effective writer and as a person who was willing to go outside the written job description.

Another friend recently offered to fill in for a coworker whose father was hospitalized with an emergency illness. The friend worked through lunchtime for one week learning how to do the minimal requirements of the other job so that customers who called in would get the attention they deserved. The temporary assignment only lasted eight work days, but it left a permanent impression on the coworker, their mutual supervisor, and other department managers. Customers got the best reward of all: business as close to normal as possible, quality service from someone who was ready and able to meet this need.

Let the right people know you can be counted on to do your best every time. Make sure your boss and other managers in the company talk about you as a person who does the right things right the first time, that you regularly produce quality results on time and within budget. Making your boss and your department look good can really enhance your reputation. Make yourself needed by others in the organization, bring value to your company, and pay appropriate attention to your relationships with key individuals around you. These political actions will help you build strong alliances and partnerships.

It's a Wrap

✔ Develop appropriate political actions. Be sensitive to the concerns of powerful stakeholder groups within your organization. Make alliances/partnerships with members of other departments.

✔ Prioritize your work relationships. Establish close connections with those who can help you accomplish your goals and objectives, rather than on the basis of social preference.

✔ Network with others who have the power or status to help you with your current projects and future career interests. Create a wider social base by seeking advice from acknowledged experts and accomplished veterans who can provide you with the resources, information, or support you need to help meet your goals or survive a crisis. Join professional associations to expand your horizons and your list of contacts.

✔ Always conduct yourself in such a way that people with power respect and like you. Create and maintain a positive image. Don't badmouth others or criticize people in public. Don't burn bridges even when it would feel good to do so.

✔ Productive partnerships are based on your willingness to recognize, appreciate, and provide what others need from you while maintaining or improving our own performance.

CHAPTER 4

POLITICAL TECHNIQUE 2
Establish Collaborative Relationships with Peers

I'm not the smartest fellow in the world, but I can sure pick smart colleagues.—**Franklin D. Roosevelt**

You can make more friends in two months by becoming interested in other people than you can in two years by trying to get people interested in you.—**Dale Carnegie**

Do I Need to Read This Chapter?

➜ How do you determine who your key constituents are?

➜ Which internal or external customers require your special attention and why?

➜ What people and departments do you depend on most to accomplish your work goals?

Doing your job is not just about getting the work done. It is also about building relationships for the future. Your success often depends on your ability to influence or persuade others to cooperate with you. A good place to start is in your own department. You can then expand your frame of reference to include other departments who depend on you for information or service and other departments you depend on to get your job done.

It is surprising how little some people know about their companies. You may have received some information from a formal orientation session, from annual reports or company newsletters, or from informal conversations with veteran employees. However, if you are still unsure about any of the following topics, take responsibility to find out as much as you can about these important facets of the company you work for.

- Its history, growth, and economic challenges
- Its current mission or purpose
- Its organizational structure including a big-picture perspective of how key departments relate to each other
- Its key functions and managers
- Its management philosophy as written and as practiced
- Its current products and services, as well as any that were discontinued and any that are in development
- Its facilities, including the layout of the building in which you work and the location of any other offices or plants

It helps to get to know your company's culture by asking yourself, "How do things really get done around here?" The answer to this question may reinforce ideas from the previous chapter about who has formal or informal power in your organization. The answer to this question may also give you a different perspective about your most important constituents and can help you build networks that are mutually beneficial.

Steve Foster, personnel manager for the engineering division of an international chemical company, started out in manufacturing supervision but moved into other operational areas by recognizing the need to build networks early in his career:

Many organizations today still have "functional silos" that define and limit individual growth and development. It's often difficult for people outside your own business, department, or function to know you and your capabilities. Informal networking can help break down some of the barriers. It's great if you are comfortable asking someone for help: "Who should I talk to about getting into sales?" It's even better if an experienced, veteran employee is willing to help you out: "Next time you're in the Home Office, give me a call and I'll introduce you to someone in sales." It's good to have an innate curiosity that lets you go beyond your own functional boundary. I've gotten involved in things I never thought I'd be doing. With support and encouragement from my boss, I developed competencies I never dreamed possible.

Carol Tunstall, a human resource manager for Rohm and Haas Company, encourages her colleagues to develop alliances with people who have an investment in your success. In other words, if you look good, they will look good, too.

Get to know who has influence in your area. I have had "informal" mentors, many of them my boss or the manager of a division. My relationship was based on that person seeing something in me, and my ability to trust that person's interest in my career and my professional development. My best mentors are honest with me because they want me to succeed.

In his book *Love and Profit: The Art of Caring Leadership* (Morrow, 1991), James A. Autry describes important bonds people form with each other at work.

By invoking the metaphor of community, we imply that we in business are bound by a fellowship of endeavor in which we commit to mutual goals, in which we contribute to the best of our abilities, in which each contribution is recognized and credited, in which there is a forum for all voices to be heard, in which our success contributes to the success of the common enterprise and to the success of others, in which we can disagree and hold differing viewpoints without withdrawing from the community and in which we take care of each other.

Expand your horizons by broadening your own cultural, educational, and professional background. If you value diversity, you will be open to new experiences and new information available in your interactions with key constituents who will often have different life experiences and cultural beliefs. Appreciate the individual differences that you and others bring to your work relationships. A different perspective, a radical approach, a slightly shaded nuance, a dramatic new direction—variety like that can salt the stew and bring out the best in everyone. Respecting others earns their respect for you and helps you accomplish together what you could not have accomplished on your own.

Quick Tips

Q: Who are your major constituents or stakeholders? Who benefits from, depends on, or expects a certain level of quality from the work that you do?

A: Use Fig. 4.1 to make a short list of the six or eight most important people who receive some product, outcome, or information from you. Your list may include external customers, peers in other departments (internal customers), direct reports who depend on you for direction or assistance, managers above you who need accurate data for strategic planning, or anyone else who would be significantly affected if you did not do your current work satisfactorily.

Q: What do these constituents need from you?

A: Use Fig. 4.1 to define some of your constituents' needs. This list may be as varied as your previous list. Each constituent probably has some unique requirement. Where one may need timely information, another may need thorough and careful documentation. Where one may want the highest quality at the best price, another may need a quick solution at the lowest possible cost. The challenge is to determine exactly what your constituents need or want from you. If you do not know for sure, the best thing is to ask them.

Q: What can you do to make your constituents and stakeholders feel valued?

A: Listen to what they have to say and act on the information they give you. Respond to what they tell you by building relationships based on trust, mutual respect, and a personal commitment to provide the highest possible level of professional service you can. That means being the best you can be at whatever people are depending on you to do for them. Use Fig. 4.2 to list the three things you need to be providing your key constituents right now.

Remember that other departments are not likely to offer their support, help, or resources for your efforts unless they see some value for them. Helping other departments understand what's in it for them, or why it's in their best interest to support your projects or initiatives, takes political know-how and timely communication.

Your Key Constituents	Their Needs
1. _____	_____
2. _____	_____
3. _____	_____
4. _____	_____
5. _____	_____
6. _____	_____
7. _____	_____
8. _____	_____

Figure 4.1

YOUR CURRENT COMMITMENTS TO MEET YOUR CONSTITUENTS' NEEDS

List the 3 primary contributions you must make to meet your most important constituents' most important needs:

1. _____

2. _____

3. _____

Figure 4.2

Danger!

- One of the risks you take by expanding your horizon or your sphere of influence is that others may perceive you as a maverick or an intruder on their turf. Make sure, therefore, that you can demonstrate the value to them of sharing information or resources with you. You may need to remind other work groups that sometimes an opposing view or a different perspective can help redefine an issue and open up discussion about a wider range of possible opportunities or solutions.

Rosemary Adiletto, prevention program coordinator for a private nonprofit organization, highlights the importance of collaboration.

So much of the prevention work in nonprofit depends on getting funds. Because I came from a funding agency, one of those groups who used to monitor my current organization, I was seen as the enemy. I needed to build collaboration, find ways to benefit my current organization. People didn't trust me or believe in what I was doing. It was new to them, and I had to show them the benefits of what I could do. For example, they had been trying to do things with a local youth center, and I knew how to do educational things with kids, so I was able to offer a service they found valuable. When you are changing jobs, you need to use relationships from the past without saying "at our old place" or "in my previous job we did such and such." You need to take an approach that says: "Here's what I do— how can that benefit you?"

Get Started

1. Be accessible. Let people know how to get in touch with you whenever they need you. Having an open-door policy at work is not good enough if you are never in your office or work area. Let key constituents know all the ways they can contact you whenever they have a serious question or concern. If people start to abuse your offer by calling you inappropriately, you can discuss a better way to handle their emergencies. The initial message is crucial: "You are important to me, and I am available when you need me."

2. Listen to what your constituents have to say. Pay attention. Ask questions to clarify and verify your understanding. Paraphrase or repeat what they are telling you until you know for sure that you are clear about their meaning. The best way you have to show people you respect them and value their ideas is by *really* listening.

3. Give your constituents the time they need to brag about their successes, worry about their work-related problems, and discuss their differences of opinion. Every conversation you have is an opportunity for you to learn more about the key people you interact with regularly at work. Giving them your time and your attention will help you know more about their needs, interests, values, and concerns—all vital information for you to use in building and maintaining your relationships with them.

4. Ask for feedback about your performance from people who can give you honest, accurate, and timely information. When you get their feedback, be appreciative (not defensive) and willing to act on it (not

Continued

ready to kill the messenger). If others see that you are interested in knowing what they have to tell you, two-way communication will be much easier for them and more useful for you.

5. Ask questions when you need to clarify or expand your understanding of someone's feedback to you. Try not to assume you know what someone means. If you are not sure, get things straightened out the first time.

6. Keep your commitments and expect others to do the same. Maintaining high personal standards can set an example for others and can help establish your reputation as a valued team player who lives up to a strong code of professionalism.

7. Establish and maintain a reputation as an expert in your area of the business. You don't have to be the best (although that would certainly help). But being recognized as someone who really knows what's going on can give you the leverage you need to influence others, even when you do not have formal authority or power.

8. Develop your interpersonal skills. Be willing to work with others toward win-win solutions that get you the best results while meeting the other person's needs as well. Think of negotiating as mutual problem solving, not a get-what-you-can-and-run proposition. Any attempt at manipulation, coercion, dishonesty, or deceit will come back to haunt and hurt you later. Playing fair works. Treating others with respect brings good results today and sets a standard for anyone who wants to work with you in the future.

One way to develop collaborative relationships is by being a team player. A team is a group of people committed to achieving a common purpose that will require each member's individual contribution and mutual cooperation. The extent to which people trust, support, respect, and feel comfortable with each other influences how well they work together. Figure 4.3 lists qualities that are often used to describe effective teams. You may want to put a plus sign (+) in front of any area where you are currently making a contribution to your team and a minus sign (–) in front of any area where you can do better. Use this self-assessment activity to help identify ways you can be a better team player.

CHARACTERISTICS OF EFFECTIVE TEAMS

- **Appropriate Leadership.** The team leader has the skills and intention to develop a team approach. Leadership of the team is seen as a shared function. Individuals other than the team leader are given the opportunity to exercise leadership when their skills are appropriate to the needs of the team.

- **Suitable Membership.** Team members are qualified and capable of contributing a "mix" of skills and characteristics that provide an appropriate balance.

- **Commitment to the Team.** Team members feel a sense of individual commitment to the aims and purposes of their team. They are willing to devote personal energy to supporting other team members. When working outside the team boundaries, the members feel a sense of belonging to and representing the team.

- **Constructive Climate.** The team has developed a climate in which people feel relaxed, able to be direct and open, and prepared to take risks.

- **Concern with Achievement.** The team is clear about its objectives, which are felt to be worthwhile. It sets targets of performance that are felt to be challenging but achievable. Energy is mainly devoted to the achievement of results, and team performance is reviewed frequently to see where improvements can be made.

- **Clear Corporate Role.** The team has a distinct and productive role within the overall organization.

- **Effective Work Methods.** The team has developed systematic and effective ways to solve problems together.

Continued

- **Well-Organized Team Procedures.** Roles are clearly defined, communication patterns are well-developed, and administrative procedures support the team's approach.

- **Honest Feedback.** Team and individual errors and weaknesses are examined, without personal attack, to enable the group to learn from its experiences.

- **Well-Developed Individuals.** Team members are deliberately developed and the team can cope with strong individual contributions.

- **Creative Strength.** The team has the capacity to create new ideas through the interactions of its members. Some innovative risk-taking is rewarded, and the team will support new ideas from individual members or from outside. Good ideas are followed through into action.

- **Positive Intergroup Relations.** Relationships with other teams have been developed to provide open personal contact and identify where working together may give maximum payoff. There is regular review of shared or collective priorities with other teams.

Figure 4.3

Personality clashes or bad chemistry between even two team members can have a significant negative impact on the whole team and its pursuit of a common goal. An effective team values and capitalizes on the diverse skills, interests, and perspectives of individual team members. An effective team develops ways to deal with the inevitable conflicts that arise when people are encouraged to disagree, and team members determine how to balance their strengths and weaknesses to make their team as successful as possible.

Don't Forget

● Conflict is inevitable and healthy if you deal with it effectively. Conflict can be an opportunity for new ideas, creativity, openness, and better rapport. Try to stay focused on the nature and causes of the conflict, not on personalities or finding someone to blame. Stay as objective as possible and identify ways to negotiate, compromise, or collaborate your way to a mutually acceptable resolution.

To be a good team player, you must first determine the role you are expected to play on the team. Usually, team members are selected on the basis of some *functional* role: you bring certain technical expertise to the team based on your past education, training, or work experience. There is a need on the team for some specialized knowledge, technique, procedure, or process, and you have the background to make a specific contribution.

If your team is your own work group or a group within your own department, others on your team may have similar expertise or technical skills. Pooling your resources and common experiences may help you improve efficiency and effectiveness. If your team is cross-functional or interdepartmental, you may be the only one with your specific functional competency. In those cases, you will be the expert that others depend on for your special knowledge or skill.

Regardless of your functional role, you will also play important *process* roles on your team. These roles vary from situation to situation, and they depend on the interpersonal behaviors you use to help the team move forward to meet its common goal. In some cases, you may focus attention on the task at hand and encourage others to do what has to be done to get results on time and within budget. In other cases, you may focus attention on how the team is working together and encourage others to reflect on relationships, interactions, and the way team members are dealing with problems, decisions, or conflict.

Effective teams achieve a healthy balance between focusing on task accomplishments (*what* gets done) and team relationships (*how* the task gets done). This allows the team not only to achieve success but also to share a sense of accomplishment about what it has taken to succeed. There are a variety of specific roles and behaviors associated with the way team members interact with each other to accomplish their purpose. When you are focused on task accomplishment, you may do any or all of the following things.

- Initiate action by proposing a task, defining a problem, suggesting a solution, recommending an idea or a procedure.
- Request information by asking for suggestions or ideas, seeking data or examples, requesting conformation or clarification.
- Give information by offering suggestions or ideas, presenting data or examples, providing confirmation or clarification.
- Test progress by making critical assessments of new ideas or recommendations, evaluating team productivity or efficiency, reminding the team of deadlines, budgets, and commitments.
- Summarize by restating ideas or conclusions after team discussions, paraphrasing a decision for the team to accept or reject, pulling together related ideas for the team to review.

When you are focused on team relationships, you may do any or all of the following things.

- Encourage others to participate.
- Recognize others for their contributions.
- Open up discussions so that others feel comfortable contributing their ideas.
- Ask opinions, feelings, and suggestions so that others know their ideas are valued.

- Suggest procedures for dealing with team problems, conflicts, or decisions.

- Clarify ideas or suggestions, help clear up any confusion, and seek consensus.

- Reduce tension by pressing for harmony and an objective evaluation of interpersonal differences.

- Suggest workable compromises in the best interest of the team.

- Collaborate with others and set an example of how people can work together.

- Build relationships with other team members based on trust and mutual respect.

Effective teams operate at peak efficiency when members balance both task and process roles and when these roles become the responsibility of all of the members. These roles are also not mutually exclusive. Very often, when performing a task role (like summarizing options for action), you may also be playing a process role (like expressing the feelings of certain team members). It does not generally matter who plays what roles, as long as the appropriate behaviors are demonstrated and balanced among team members at appropriate times. Effective teams often distribute responsibilities across the team, with members voluntarily assuming roles they are most confident and competent at performing. Think about the teams you currently belong to and make sure you are doing your fair share.

Danger!

- Building relationships for the future is an important part of doing your job. Remember, however, that your primary responsibility is to get your current work done first. Don't let networking and relationship building for the future become a substitute for getting your current work done efficiently and effectively.

To be an effective team player, focus first on the task at hand and determine what tangible results you can produce for the team. Identify operational outcomes that will have the greatest impact: improved sales, faster delivery time, safer procedures, reduced development time, improved customer satisfaction, better inventory control, reduced costs or expenses, improved quality. Concentrate on personal contributions that can or will affect the bottom line for your team, your department, or the organization. By improving profits, productivity, or your company's competitive position, you do more than anything else to help ensure your team's success. If you do those things in a respectful, collaborative, considerate way—without manipulating, embarrassing, or threatening other team members—you will be able to successfully balance both your task and your process team roles.

Don't Forget

- Both personal and team goals are achieved through mutual trust, respect, and support. Very little that is worth much is accomplished by getting what you want at someone else's expense. If you are trustworthy, others will feel comfortable expressing their ideas, feelings, disagreements, and opinions. If you are perceived as untrustworthy, others will withhold important information, values, and perspectives that otherwise can be valuable input for you.

Everyone likes to work with someone who is cooperative, helpful, friendly, and upbeat. No one likes to work with someone who is cynical, mean-spirited, negative, and disgruntled. Complimenting coworkers on their good work can help build strong relationships with them. Giving people encouragement and positive feedback goes a long way to establishing a productive and comfortable work environment for everyone. Offering your coworkers information, strategies, support, and solutions that will be mutually beneficial can help establish long-lasting relationships that will make life more productive for everyone.

According to Katherine Huston, responding to the requests of coworkers starts with a quick assessment of her ability (not her availability) to do what they are asking her to do.

> If someone says to me, "Are you able to do such and such," and I have the skills, I always say yes, and then I add, "I believe I can do that if I have time to research the particular subject matter and get back to you with some specifics," or "With the projects I have in front of me now, I can do it, but I won't be able to get to it until next week," or "I'd be happy to take a look at that and see how it will fit into the overall plan." It's saying yes in a certain way so that the first thing people hear is something that supports what they believe is needed.

Joseph Toto, a Hoffmann-LaRoche executive, remembers learning an important lesson from an incident early in his career.

> Sometimes coworkers can say things behind the scenes which can influence your own common boss. In one of my earlier jobs, for example, I was asked to audit my peers—the same people I needed to work with every day. I needed to be careful, professional, and respectful with their sensitive information. It was a delicate situation that had some unique opportunities and created a ripple effect that I knew would help or hurt me build extended relationships. On another occasion, when I was about to do a task for the first time, I reached out to someone who had done the same task many times in the past. I asked her to be a copresenter at a high-visibility meeting. She thanked me, but encouraged me to do it by myself as a new person needing the opportunity to establish my own credibility. She trusted me, I acknowledged her in my comments, and after that, we worked together successfully for a long time.

Good teamwork depends on good communication. To be an effective team player, you need to sharpen your basic communication skills. When you need to *request* information, ask yourself questions like:

Shortcuts

Here are a few quick ways to widen your information base and expand your sphere of influence.

- Ask people who are involved in the processes or projects you want to know more about to share their information and expertise with you.

- Offer to brainstorm with others so that you can share your ideas and listen to theirs. Talk to others about your ideas and accept their input and suggestions.

- Network with key people. Build formal and informal relationships that allow you to exchange information and develop channels of support. Professional organizations, alumni associations, community groups, and service clubs are good sources of networking opportunities.

- What do you need to know and who has the information you need?

- What is the best (fastest, clearest, easiest) way for you to get the information you need?

- When and why do you need the information?

When you need to *receive* information, ask yourself questions like:

- What do you need to do to ensure that you get timely, accurate, and complete information from others?

- How do you let others know they can give you the information you need even if it is bad news or difficult feedback?

- What steps do you need to take to strengthen your interpersonal relationships with key people you depend on for information?

When you need to *give* information to others, ask yourself questions like:

- What do you need to do to ensure that your communication is timely, accurate, and complete?

- What facts or examples can you use to ensure that your communication is data-based and objective?

- What is the best way (time, place, method) for you to give information to people above you in the organization?

- What is the best way for you to communicate with coworkers, direct reports, customers, suppliers, or any other key people you interact with on a regular basis?

Effective team players know how to get what they want without hurting themselves or others. They have identified their individual strengths and continue to capitalize on them.

Here are a few strategies you can use to become a more effective team player.

- Share information with others who will benefit from knowing what you know. If you are not certain whether a piece of information is important to a coworker, let them decide: "I heard something about your project that I thought you should know" or "Would you be interested in this magazine article I read recently about computer software?" Offers like this can help establish your reputation as a person who keeps in touch with others about their interests or needs and is willing to pass along data that can be useful to them. Any time you write a report or document the results of one of your projects, make a list of everyone who can benefit from your work. You probably have a short list of people who need to know what you have done, but a longer list can include some of your peers who might like to know what you have accomplished or decided. Consider circulating proposals, customer correspondence, consulting reports, and any other documents that others might find valuable. Giving your associates copies of useful memos, leaving someone a helpful e-mail note, giving one of your peers a heads-up warning about a meeting or new company initiative—all of these collaborative efforts demonstrate your willingness to be a team player.

- Compliment others for their efforts and good work. Be sincere and factual. Sometimes a simple "Thank you for getting that information to me so quickly" can make another person's day. Stating your appreciation or noticing a peer's contribution shows that you are interested in their work and your relationship with them. Often, in the rush of our daily lives, we forget to pass on an encouraging word to someone who could use a lift or a positive remark. Sometimes asking a coworker's advice can be a nice way to compliment them for their expertise or performance: "I know you have made several successful presentations recently, and I was wondering if you would be willing to give me a few tips," or "Congratulations on your recent accomplishment. How did you do it?" Giving peers an opportunity to brag a little about their good work reinforces your interest in working together in a cooperative atmosphere based on a commonly shared belief that teamwork is better than competition or isolationism. You and your associates are working together toward a common goal, and opportunities to support each other should not be minimized or ignored. A few positive comments can help others around you keep their problems in perspective. You can help maintain a spirit of cooperation that is an important characteristic of all successful teams.

- Help streamline work processes. Keep things moving smoothly from your work area to the next. If you see a potential or actual bottleneck, do your best to remove any obstacles that may adversely affect your team's efforts. Get help as quickly as possible. Keep others informed about any pending delays or other problems. Communicate with anyone who needs to know when your part of the work is slowing down or going off track. Do not hesitate to ask for suggestions or resources from peers who might have a better, more objective perspective on ways to improve your work.

- Share credit for your successes with anyone who has helped you. Letting your superiors know about the contributions others have made to your work projects will reinforce their impression of you as a team player and will strengthen your coworkers' opinion of you as a person who enjoys collaboration. Peers will be more willing to work with you, support your ongoing efforts, and ask your help on their projects when you go out of your way to give them credit for their assistance. Conversely, if a particular project does not go as well as you expected, be sure you are willing to accept your share of the blame. Again, acknowledging that, good or bad, you and others are working together on most of your assignments will build relationships and ensure that you are regarded as a valued team member with team leadership potential.

- Offer your opinions and give others useful, data-based information that will help them maintain or improve their current performance. Sometimes called *peer coaching,* this strategy requires sensitivity to the feelings of your coworkers. Careful, thoughtful planning can help you present your views in a way that the receiver will find beneficial. The other person must understand, accept, and be able to act on your feedback. To make this process work, try to use specific details and examples, talk to people when they are most receptive to hearing from you, allow adequate time to discuss your feedback, and reach agreement about the purpose and content of your message. If you frame your coaching in the right language, so that the other person sees the value of your insights, you will demonstrate that you are interested in developing an effective work relationship with them and that you are interested in hearing their suggestions about your performance. Giving and getting feedback can improve teamwork. Sharing your perceptions is the only way you can modify someone else's perceptions of you. If you are tactful and diplomatic, you can keep even your most critical observations constructive and ensure that your honest feedback is appreciated and used.

Remember that, within your own work environment, you have the opportunity and ability to collaborate with others in a way that will help you be successful. To expand your sphere of influence, you need to develop relationships built on mutual respect and cooperation. By communicating your willingness to help others succeed, you will create a positive work environment and establish a reputation for yourself as a team player.

Collaborating with others can bring you and them many benefits.

- Collaboration establishes interdependence. It is nonthreatening. When people recognize the value of giving or getting help, and realize it is expected, they will work together with you to reach your common goal.
- Collaboration builds commitment, ownership, and satisfaction. People can see the results of their work and share credit for the team's accomplishments.
- Collaboration sets the stage for future performance. Productivity improves when people learn from past mistakes, celebrate current successes, and modify outdated procedures in response to changing conditions.

When people work together they push each other to higher levels of achievement. New ideas are suggested, tested, and implemented. Synergy occurs: what the team accomplishes is greater than the combined efforts of team members working individually.

It's a Wrap

✔ Your success depends on your ability to influence or persuade others to cooperate with you.

✔ Be a team player. Offer your coworkers information and support that will help them. People you help will tell others, and your network will grow as good news about you spreads.

✔ Learn how to communicate for results. Decide what information you need to do your job in a timely and cost-effective way, then determine who has the information you need, how you can get additional information when you need it, and how you can improve the way you get information.

✔ Decide what information you have that will help others do their jobs more effectively, then determine what you can do to improve the way you give them this information. Communication is the key to effective collaboration.

▬◆▬◆▬◆▬◆▬◆▬◆▬◆▬◆▬◆▬◆▬◆▬◆▬◆▬◆▬◆▬

CHAPTER 5

POLITICAL TECHNIQUE 3
Know and Contribute to Your Company's Strategic Objectives

◆▬◆▬◆▬◆▬◆▬◆▬◆▬◆▬◆▬◆▬◆▬◆▬◆▬◆▬◆▬◆▬◆

The way to achieve success is first to have a definite, clear, practical ideal—a goal, an objective. Second, have the necessary means to achieve your ends—wisdom, money, materials, and methods. Third, adjust all your means to that end.—**Aristotle**

Men and women want to do a good job, and if they are provided the proper environment, they will do so.—**Bill Hewlett, Founder, Hewlett-Packard**

Do I Need to Read This Chapter?

→ Do you know specifically what your company expects from you?

→ How will you know if you are making a contribution to your company's success?

→ How do your manager and others measure your performance and your value to the company?

An organization is only as good as the processes it uses to meet its objectives. You need to be sure that your work processes are meeting your constituents' needs and that those processes work effectively and efficiently. You need to be sure that the objectives you are working on are driven by your customers' needs and the organization's requirements.

The thought process behind setting objectives is often described as a cascade of critical information that answers these questions.

- What is the organization's purpose?
- What is your department's or team's purpose?
- What part do you play on your team?
- What do you need to achieve?
- How will you know you are effective and successful?

You and your manager can use this downward funneling technique to focus on specific team and individual objectives in a way that ensures your work is connected to and aligned with broader, big-picture corporate objectives.

Get Started

1. Review your company's mission statement and strategic objectives.

2. Review your department's mission statement and strategic objectives.

3. Develop your own business goals by focusing on how you can contribute to organizational and departmental priorities.

4. Discuss how you think you can make a contribution with your immediate supervisor and reach agreement about your short-term goals and priorities.

5. Communicate your goals and priorities to those who need to know about them.

6. Periodically review your progress with your supervisor and anyone else who needs to know.

7. Revise your goals and priorities when necessary to make sure you are making a timely and meaningful contribution.

8. Demonstrate your commitment to important corporate or departmental initiatives and objectives.

Setting objectives requires effective two-way communication so that important information flows upward, downward, and across the organization. Another way to look at alignment, therefore, is to ask a series of related *what/how/who* questions. The answers to these questions should produce a chain of related activities that will help you make certain you are contributing to important corporate objectives. Each of your major activities should state clearly:

- The goal for that activity (the *what*).

- The work process, procedure, or technique (the *how*) that delivers the result identified in the goal.

- The measures to be used to evaluate progress and success (*how* we assess *what* we have accomplished).

- The resources (the *who*) needed to achieve the desired or required results.

When you work with your immediate supervisor to set individual objectives, you are working together to clarify key performance areas and to reach agreement about what you are expected to accomplish during a defined time period. Objectives are mutually agreed upon performance outcomes. Objectives help you understand what you have to do to ensure that your actions and priorities are in alignment with company goals. In *The Practice of Management*, Peter Drucker describes objectives as: "the instrument panel necessary to pilot the business enterprise. Without them management flies by the seat of its pants—without landmarks to steer by, without maps and without having flown the route before."

It is politically smart for you to be sure that your objectives are summarized and written down. Writing them will help you understand and remember them. Your written objectives then become a working document that you and your supervisor can use throughout the year for coaching, feedback, and progress reports. Your annual objectives are not intended to be your complete job description. They are the most important areas necessary for you to focus on, and you should review, discuss, and revise them regularly.

Setting objectives with your supervisor will help you accomplish the following.

- Achieve your individual and team objectives.
- Ensure alignment with broader corporate objectives.
- Clarify expectations about duties, responsibilities, assignments, and priorities.
- Provide a method and system for coaching and performance-based feedback.
- Identify your individual strengths and interests.
- Keep your current job challenging and interesting.

When you and your supervisor write objectives, usually near the beginning of the year, you know your objectives are more likely to be aligned with corporate and departmental objectives. When you and your supervisor revise objectives throughout the year, you know you are working on current priorities.

Quick Tips

Q: What results does your organization need from you and your area of responsibility?

A: There are a number of critical outcomes you are being paid to deliver. Read your job description and discuss your current duties and responsibilities with your immediate supervisor and anyone else who has influence over your job performance.

Q: What activities must be done to get the results you need?

A: Once you have defined required or desired results, determine specific actions, techniques, and behaviors that will help you deliver expected outcomes. Your list may include special projects, temporary assignments, new priorities, or the routine activities you do every day to meet your company's expectations and earn your paycheck.

Q: What contributions does your organization rely on you to make? What are you really getting paid to do?

A: Make sure you are doing the right things right the first time. Check to be sure that things you enjoy doing or are comfortable doing are still what the company needs from you. Doing something out of habit or because you have always done it in a particular way may not be the best way now.

Q: With whom do you need to coordinate your efforts to achieve your desired results?

A: Know your key constituents and customers. Make sure you are providing results to people who depend on you. Include on this list your manager, your coworkers, your customers, your direct reports, and anyone else you interact with on a regular basis.

Many managers use objectives to:

- Allocate resources.
- Give recognition for work well done.
- Review and adjust priorities to meet changes in the business.
- Establish a starting point for coaching and performance-based feedback.

You can use objectives to:

- Understand what is expected of you.
- Track your own performance and progress.
- Control what you do and how you do it.

Danger!

- Remember that personal goals are goals you do not get paid to accomplish. They provide direction for getting the things you want in life like family, career, social, and self-development objectives. Business goals are goals you get paid to accomplish. They are the results your organization expects from you—the unique contributions you make when you go to work each day. Try to maintain a balance between the two.

In *The Empowered Manager* (Jossey-Bass, 1988), Peter Block recommends putting the organization's objectives ahead of personal ambition.

Genuine, long-term self-interest, though typically defined as doing those things that will get us to the top, is better served if we act first and foremost to serve the organization and make our own personal ascension the second priority. This is not an issue of morality but a practical path to empowerment. Being driven to serve the organization is the essence of enlightened self-interest. It is also at the heart of positive politics.

Carol Tunstall offers this advice.

You need to look continually to the future and understand what trends, experience, and skills will be strategic to your organization or profession. Understand, also, which jobs or responsibilities might be outsourced by your current company. Don't become obsolete. Know what's going on inside your company (objectives, strategic plans, and proposed initiatives) and outside the company (through conferences, symposiums, books, and both local and national professional organizations). Expand your understanding beyond your own technical or functional areas. Learn how to link with other functions.

You need to understand what is expected of you so that your actions are aligned with company, departmental, and team objectives. You share responsibility with your supervisor to ensure that the alignment is clear. High performance comes when you understand clearly what you have to do and when you have challenging performance objectives. The most frequent cause of poor performance is a lack of clarity about what is expected, not a lack of skills or a willingness to contribute.

Don't Forget

- Plan for success. Determine how you will allocate your resources (time, money, and energy) using a thoughtful and comprehensive strategy. Chart a path that points the way to personal and professional success. Decide which actions or activities will move you closer to achieving your short-term and long-term goals.

Setting objectives is a continuous process in which you work together with your supervisor to identify key business processes; determine priorities, measures, and targets; define cross-functional or team objectives; and clarify individual, personal goals for the year.

The process should allow for flexibility and adaptability; it should be based on real work that encourages commitment and accountability. Many people have found the mnemonic SMART helpful in developing and discussing good objectives.

S pecific
M easurable
A chievable
R elevant
T ime-Bound

A performance requirement is *specific* if it states what is to be done and describes behaviors which can be seen as leading to the attainment of the objective. The activities necessary to achieve the goal need not be listed or discussed unless you find doing so useful or necessary.

A goal should be *measurable*. How well something is done might reflect on its timeliness, accuracy, cost, and completeness. While some jobs lend themselves more easily to quantitative analysis, all objectives should be framed so that you can determine reasonably whether and to what extent they have been reached. There are different types of measurements:

- *Results measures* tell you and others what work is getting done. They are used to monitor the outputs of the work process so that these outputs meet customer or company requirements. These measures focus on outcomes, deliverables, or accomplishments such as total sales, on-time shipments, or number of new products. They give you hard data about your output and your delivery of desired or required results.

- *Process measures* indicate how work is getting done. They are used to ensure that you are doing what has to be done to achieve the desired outcomes. To develop process measures you first identify the desired result and then define what you need to do to reach this result.

Results measures show *whether* you are actually giving the organization and your customers what they want. Process measures show *how* your processes are working to give the organization and your customers what they want.

Don't Forget

- Monitor and measure your progress and your accomplishments. Use established benchmarks, target dates, or schedules to determine how well you are moving toward accomplishing your desired goals.

An objective must not be unreachable or beyond what could reasonably be expected of you. Performance requirements should be *achievable,* but they should also challenge you and encourage you to give the most of your talent, ability, and energy. You should feel comfortable discussing with your supervisor whether you have the authority, resources, and capability to achieve a particular objective.

All performance objectives should be *relevant*—selected because they support the mission, purpose, and strategy of the organization and the particular division or unit within your organization. Ideally, you should review your objectives with your supervisor or manager after department objectives have cascaded down from higher levels in the company. You should also have a clear idea about your priorities. Figure 5.1 illustrates a fairly common way of defining the

---

ESTABLISHING PRIORITIES

IMPORTANCE

5 = Critical to your success

4 = Necessary to your success

3 = Important to your success

2 = Helpful to your success

1 = Minimal impact on your success

URGENCY

5 = Must be done this month

4 = Should be done this month

3 = Must be done this quarter

2 = Should be done this quarter

1 = Must be done by year-end

IMPORTANCE × URGENCY = PRIORITY

"A" Priority = 16 to 25

"B" Priority = 8 to 15

"C" Priority = 6 to 1

Figure 5.1

importance and the urgency of a goal so that you can give it an appropriate priority rating.

An objective should be *time-bound*—an activity, task, or process that must be completed by a particular date, on a regular schedule, or on a routine basis. You should know when or how often specific tasks need to be completed.

Don't Forget

- Celebrate your successes. If you have fallen short, modify your approach using new learnings or information.

Finally, objectives should be discussed and documented so that you can receive, understand, and act on feedback about the results of your performance. A self-monitoring system allows for ongoing evaluation, improvement, and development. You and your immediate supervisor share responsibility for maintaining alignment and achieving success. SMART objectives set the stage for future conversations.

Use the worksheet in Fig. 5.2 to practice writing one of your most important objectives using the SMART guidelines. Then use the worksheet in Fig. 5.3 to define your three or four most important goals or objectives.

Once you have listed all of your business goals, here are some questions to help you prioritize them:

1. Of all the goals you've written, which are the most valuable or significant to you?

2. Which goals are most supportive of your company's mission, purpose, and strategic objectives?

3. If you could accomplish only three or four of your goals, which ones would you work on?

WRITING YOUR OBJECTIVES USING SMART GUIDELINES

Specific—What are you trying to produce or accomplish and how? _____

_____

Measurable—How will you know you have accomplished the objective or that you are moving in the right direction? _____

_____

Achievable—What resources and authority do you need? _____

_____

Relevant—How will this objective affect company or department activities? _____

_____

Time-Bound—When or how often does this objective need to be accomplished? ____

_____

Figure 5.2

4. Which of your goals will yield the highest payoff, first of all to your company and then to you?

5. What would happen if you don't achieve these goals? What would be the negative consequences for you and for your company?

6. Would failure to achieve any one of these goals cause you to get fired, demoted, transferred, or held back from future promotions?

Figure 5.4 lists several questions that you can use to double-check the quality of your current goals. Figure 5.5 lists several questions that you can use to double-check the priority you have assigned a specific goal. Use these checklists as self-assessment tools to make sure that you are emphasizing the right things in your current job.

GOAL-SETTING WORKSHEET

GOAL DESCRIPTION

What? _____

For Whom?_____

When? _____

Priority? _____

GOAL DESCRIPTION

What? _____

For Whom? _____

When? _____

Priority? _____

GOAL DESCRIPTION

What? _____

For Whom? _____

When? _____

Priority? _____

GOAL DESCRIPTION

What? _____

For Whom? _____

When? _____

Priority? _____

Figure 5.3

KEY QUESTIONS FOR DETERMINING THE QUALITY OF GOALS

- Does the goal statement describe a key result and a target date?
- Is the goal measurable and verifiable, and do you have responsibility for final results?
- Does the goal relate to one of your key job responsibilities? Is the goal truly significant or really routine?
- Does the goal relate to one of your company's functional objectives or current strategies?
- Can the goal be understood by others involved in implementation?
- Is the goal realistic and attainable, but also challenging?
- Will the result, when achieved, justify the effort required to achieve it? Is there a cost-to-benefit payoff?
- Is the goal consistent with current policies and procedures?
- Can various performance levels or levels of accomplishment be clearly distinguished to facilitate evaluation of results?
- Is the priority rating for the goal appropriate?

Figure 5.4

Danger!

- Your goals will help you move forward in a certain direction. But not every goal should be pursued at the same speed. Once you have established a goal, you need to place a value on it. The value should be based primarily on what must be done, not on what you prefer or enjoy doing. Once you have placed a value on the goal, you have established its priority. Make sure what you think is important is consistent with what others in the organization need from you.

PRIORITY CHECKLIST

1. Is this a priority which you have attained or tried to attain in the past?
2. If yes, did you attain it: with ease? with challenge? with great difficulty?
3. If you attempted but did not attain it, why not?
   - Priority set too high
   - Not enough resources
   - Not enough skill
   - Extenuating circumstances
4. If there have been extenuating circumstances in the past, have the circumstances been corrected?
5. Have you prioritized this goal differently in the past? Higher? Lower?
6. Does the goal or priority contribute directly to your company's current priorities?
7. Does the prioritizing of your goal reflect the same importance as a company or departmental goal?
8. If this goal or priority were met, what would be the impact on:
   - Your professional development?
   - Your relationship with your team?
   - Departmental or functional goals or priorities?
   - Corporate goals or priorities?
9. If this goal or priority were *not* met, what would be the impact on:
   - Your professional development?
   - Your relationship with your team?
   - Departmental or functional goals or priorities?
   - Corporate goals or priorities?
10. Does this goal or priority contribute to the long-term growth of your company? Will it be important three to five years from now?

Figure 5.5

Remember, whatever you are trying to achieve, you cannot do it alone. Ultimately, you're responsible for what *you* accomplish and the actions *you* take every minute of every day. But this takes teamwork, getting commitments from others, and integrating your plans and actions with others. Once you have a clear action plan, therefore, it is important that you decide who will affect your plan and who will be affected by it. Ask yourself:

- Who needs to know your goals and priorities?
- Why do they need to know? Can they help you achieve success or could they interfere with your progress?
- How would you like them to collaborate with you?
- What information or help do you need from them?
- When will you need their help?
- What contingencies should you consider and discuss with them?

Don't Forget

- Anticipate problems. Incorporate into your strategic thinking both contingency planning and risk analysis. Do not dwell too long on negative possibilities, but be proactive about problems that can be avoided, managed, or minimized.

Be specific about what you expect from others. Then set realistic deadlines based on when you need their help and when they will be able to give it. Sometimes our best-laid plans fail because we have underestimated or forgotten the impact that others can have on our activities.

There are several techniques that can help you when you are trying to define or clarify objectives. One approach is to ask yourself *who, what, when, where,* and *why* questions. For example, you may want to follow this line of questioning:

1. Who is the constituent (internal or external customer) who will be affected by or involved in this objective?
2. What am I trying to achieve for this constituent/customer?
3. What does this person want or need from me? By when and for how much?
4. What measures (including feedback from the constituent/customer) will indicate that I am being successful?
5. How important or urgent is this objective? What priority am I giving this objective and why?

Maintaining alignment with corporate objectives requires knowing your constituents and your customers. As discussed in Chap. 4, this involves knowing who they are and knowing what they really want from you. To help satisfy your constituents/customers, ask yourself three key questions.

1. What do they need from you?
2. What do they do with what you give them?
3. Are there any gaps between what you give them and what they need?

As you ask these questions, keep several other issues in mind.

- Be aware of your capabilities and look for opportunities to provide a higher level of products or services.
- Check that your capabilities match your constituents/customers' requests.
- Try to please your constituents/customers by anticipating their needs and looking for ways to satisfy them more effectively and consistently.

When you know what constituents/customers want, how they use your products or services, what you can do to make these products or services more acceptable or valuable to them, and how you can respond to new needs, you begin to build relationships based on trust and mutual respect.

Shortcuts

- Make certain you contribute to current goals, initiatives, and opportunities. Stay informed about industry trends and new business possibilities.

- Be visible and vocal in your support of relevant corporate objectives. Support your company's current projects and key initiatives. Whether it is performance management, total quality leadership, empowerment, customer service excellence, pay for performance, or some other initiative, learn what you can about these corporate efforts, become a vocal supporter, and encourage others to get involved.

- Make sure that key managers know your worth and what it would cost the company if you left.

- Volunteer for special projects and assignments that interest you and that you know you can achieve. Improve your visibility and credibility by being seen as someone who has good ideas and takes timely, decisive action. Expand your areas of expertise by getting involved in tasks that broaden your experience and give you a chance to try new roles.

Years before starting her own consulting practice, Johanna Zitto found that contributing to her company's success also helped her get ahead.

I learned early in my work career to focus on what's important to the company. At one of the Macy's retail divisions, I managed nine ready-to-wear departments. In general, buyers questioned whether we store line managers knew what we were doing, and managers questioned whether buyers ever worked in stores to know firsthand why we didn't treat each buyer's department as if it were the only thing we had to do. So there was an underlying tone of tension and, in some cases, opposition. Since I was in that position less than a year (although not new to retail), I realized that if our store was going to maximize sales potential for a particular category, I would have to convince the buyer from a position of business partner, not store line adversary trying to make her look bad.

Her annual performance review was based on sales growth, stock status, and gross profits, so I linked my store's business objectives with the buyer's overall department goals in developing the new plan, careful to stick to the facts and valid business recommendations in a way that didn't blame the buyer or question her judgment. That strategy turned out to be the right approach. The report prompted a formal presentation to the buyer, the store manager, and the merchandising VP, and I eventually got promoted to be that buyer's assistant.

Joseph Toto, Hoffmann-LaRoche's director of organizational effectiveness, gives the following advice for anyone starting out in the business world today.

Balance is important. You need to be able to contribute something as soon as possible. Make your mark; add value as soon as you can. Learn the ways, needs, culture of the company you work for and begin building relationships as quickly as you can.

Peter Block describes this commitment to contribution and service as an important component of genuine, long-term self-interest.

We decide to do the things that we feel genuinely contribute to the organization and its purpose. We treat this business as if it were our own. If it were our own business, we would not want rivalry, competition, and undermining actions to take place among the units working for us. If it were our own business, we wouldn't want people doing things just to look good; we would want people doing things because they had meaning for the business and served their users.

Don't Forget

- Success is a never-ending process. As songwriter Irving Berlin once said, "The toughest thing about being a success is that you have to keep on being a success."

Peter Block calls *mastery* the final component of enlightened self-interest, or as he describes it, "simply learning as much as you can about the activity that you're engaged in. There's a pride and satisfaction in understanding your function better than anyone else and better than even you thought possible."

Make a positive impression on senior management and do not hesitate to do some modest self-promotion. Seek out opportunities to excel in front of people who have formal or informal power in your organization. Accept invitations to participate in key strategic meetings and prepare carefully so that you can make a meaningful contribution to the meeting's purpose or objective. Share your successes with your boss, but encourage your boss to share your successes with his or her superiors. Offer to send a copy of your report to someone higher in the company. Ask your supervisor if a key manager is aware that a specific project has been completed on time and within budget. Volunteer to attend a management meeting where you can discuss the outcomes and challenges of a successful project. Pass on compliments from your customers so that your supervisor at least has the chance to talk positively about your performance to others in the company. Be sure you are making significant contributions to your organization's most important objectives, and be sure the right people know how valuable you are to their company's ongoing success.

Start with your immediate supervisor, but do what you can to keep the good news about you flowing upward in the company. Establish your reputation; then use careful self-promotion techniques to ensure that others are talking positively about you. When you have a chance to talk with an influential person, make sure you use the time well. Discuss something of substance, something important that is going on in your department or in the company.

One of our colleagues used to call this practice her elevator speech. She imagined herself traveling by elevator with the president of her company from the executive offices on the tenth floor to the employee cafeteria in the basement of the building. She challenged herself to develop a two-minute introduction and description of her current projects or successes so that she was always prepared for one of these chance encounters with a key executive.

Others we know have gotten into the habit of formulating brief questions or comments about key company initiatives so they are ready and able to respond intelligently when a visiting executive stops by and asks, "How are things going?" The right answer is usually "Fine" (or another positive alternative) followed by some well-informed compliment like "especially now that the company has updated our computer system" or "since our supervisors have started encouraging team decision-making and problem-solving activities." If you can pass on a sincere compliment about something that makes your immediate supervisor look good, take advantage of the rare opportunity to say something positive to someone who probably rarely hears good news. It is even better if the executive you are talking to has had something to do with your supervisor's accomplishment—your compliment gets double mileage.

Try to remember that senior managers in your company are busy people with weighty problems. The worst thing you can do, even on a brief elevator ride or a short hallway conversation, is to dump one of your problems on them with little time for a constructive conversation. There is a time and a place for discussing and resolving problems. A brief encounter is the best time for a few positive, upbeat, encouraging words about whatever you can think of that is going well in your company today. If you cannot think of something nice to say, talk about the weather or some other innocuous topic. Better to miss an opportunity than to blow it by saying something that will leave a bad impression on someone who counts and probably will remember these few minutes with you.

Knowing what you can do to help make your organization successful and then doing it will automatically increase your value to the company. And when you increase your value to the company, you set yourself on a path for personal and professional success.

It's a Wrap

✔ Ideally, there should be a cascading effect that connects your goals with your organization's business purpose and objectives. When that happens, your business goals will support your organization's mission and purpose, and you will be able to state clearly the contributions you are making to help your organization get the results it needs.

✔ Whatever you are trying to achieve, you can't do it alone. Ultimately, you are responsible for what you accomplish and the actions you take every minute of every day. But it takes teamwork, getting commitments from others, and coordinating your plans and activities with theirs. Henry Ford described it this way, "Coming together is a beginning. Keeping together is progress. Working together is success."

◆◆◆◆◆◆◆◆◆◆◆◆◆◆◆◆◆◆◆◆◆◆◆◆◆◆◆◆◆◆◆

CHAPTER 6

POLITICAL TECHNIQUE 4
Tell the Truth

◆◆◆◆◆◆◆◆◆◆◆◆◆◆◆◆◆◆◆◆◆◆◆◆◆◆◆◆◆◆◆

To be persuasive we must be believable; to be believable we must be credible; to be credible, we must be truthful.
—**Edward R. Murrow, Journalist & News Commentator**

If you tell the truth, you don't have to remember anything.
—**Mark Twain**

Do I Need to Read This Chapter?

➡ How much credibility do you need and how much do you have with people at work?

➡ Are your actions consistent with your words? Can people depend on you?

➡ Are you comfortable giving and receiving honest feedback?

◆◆◆

Politics is not about sacrificing your values, principles, or standards. Politics should not jeopardize your integrity. In fact, you should gain respect, influence, and power by taking actions that are based on what you know is right, not what is expedient or popular. Peter Scotese, the retired CEO of Spring Industries, once said that: "Integrity is not a 90 percent thing, not a 95 percent thing; either you have it or you don't."

Integrity means being complete, whole, entire. The word comes from the Latin word *integer,* which means untouched, complete in itself, true to oneself. Build credibility and trust by making sure that others know you have integrity. People will know they can depend on you if you keep your promises and follow through on your commitments.

Your reputation for dependability is built on several basic business principles. For example, don't make promises you can't keep, and don't make promises that box in someone else. Take ownership of your actions by creating an I-you relationship with others: "I will do this for you" or "Here's how and when I can help you with that problem." Remember what you said you were going to do, then do it! Keep a tickler system, calendar, or to-do list nearby at all times. Organize your priorities by determining which tasks are most important and most urgent. Manage your time and your priorities by identifying and addressing common time wasters like the following list.

- Interruptions and distractions
- Poor communication
- Oversocializing
- Asking for help when you may not need it
- Not asking for help when you do need it
- Cluttered or messy work area

Research studies comparing supportive and defensive communication environments have determined that there are a number of things people can do to create a trusting and supportive communi-

Quick Tips

Q: Can you be trusted? Are you honest in what you say and do?

A: If you want to be perceived as trustworthy and credible, there is no such thing as occasional honesty or situational dishonesty. The truth (or the lie) will always catch up with you. Once detected, the dishonest moment can plague you forever and cast a shadow on every word you say from now on.

Q: Is what you are doing consistent with what you said you would do?

A: People should know where you stand on important issues because your actions support your words. People around you should be able to understand your values and priorities because you keep promises and follow through on your commitments.

Q: Do you communicate clearly to people who need to know what you are thinking and why you are acting in a particular way?

A: The words you use should not send mixed messages. Others should not misinterpret your suggestions or ideas as promises or commitments. Clarify and verify your messages so they are not confusing or misleading.

Q: Are you dependable?

A: There is no room for a double standard here. If you value dependability, you must make certain it is a trademark of all your working relationships. Establishing a reputation for reliability requires consistent and careful attention.

cation climate. These studies highlight how people work together in these positive, trusting atmospheres. Some of these techniques can be helpful to you when you are trying to establish or maintain a trusting work relationship:

- Use descriptive, nonevaluative speech. Acknowledge the validity of the other person's perception of the world and express your willingness to work with the other person, at least during the communication.

- Take a problem-orientation standpoint rather than trying to control the listener. A problem orientation implies a desire to collaborate in exploring a mutual problem rather than trying to alter the listener. Postpone taking sides and be more interested in solving the problem than assigning blame.

- Be spontaneous and honest rather than motivated by hidden agendas or ulterior motives. Deal with others honestly and without deception. Do not attempt to manipulate others or control them by imposing your personal attitudes on them.

- Understand the feelings of your listener, rather than appearing unconcerned or neutral about the listener's welfare. Show empathy to reassure others that you can identify with their problems.

- Show respect for the other person by being open to new ideas and not simply dominating or controlling the interaction. Value the other person's contributions and respect their self-esteem.

- Show a willingness to modify your own behavior and ideas whenever appropriate, rather than being rigid and narrow-minded. Remain open to new information. Do not give the impression that you know all the answers and do not need help from anyone.

Another critical ethical practice is *always tell the truth*. Tact and diplomacy may help you pick the right words carefully. However, deception and manipulation lead to the wrong words and the potential that you do irreparable damage to your reputation. Some experts are quick to point out that honesty does not require full disclosure as long as you are clear about areas where you are unable or uncomfortable providing detailed or complete information. If you clearly state that you would rather not discuss a particular topic, others will usually understand your concern for privacy about sensitive issues. However, the more you are willing and able to share information about yourself, the easier it will be for others to work with you. Greater disclosure between people usually leads to better working relationships and can help you resolve conflicts and solve problems more effectively.

Self-disclosure involves giving others feedback about your feelings, values, and perceptions. Feedback is verbal or nonverbal communication to a person or group about your priorities, your interests, or your reactions to their behavior. It is through feedback that others know how you see them, how you feel about what they are doing, how you are responding to their ideas or suggestions. Conversely, it is also through feedback—the kind you receive from others—that you get to know how others feel about you. By being receptive to feedback from others about how your behavior is

Get Started

1. Learn your job and do it effectively. You will earn credibility and develop confidence by demonstrating competence.

2. Ask for feedback from people who really matter to you at work—those who depend on you for results and those you depend on for your success.

3. Give feedback to people who depend on you for information about their performance. The more you are willing to be sincerely helpful to others, the more they will reciprocate and respond positively to your need for information or help.

4. Make promises you can keep and then keep them. Follow through on important commitments that you and others have defined as high priorities. If you need to delay action or take a different approach, communicate what has changed about your situation as quickly and as honestly as you can. Most people will understand an emergency change of plans, but few will tolerate lies, poor excuses, or alibis when you do not come through for them.

5. Communicate clearly what you are thinking, why you are doing certain things, and what you expect from people. The more you share with others, the easier it will be to get things done efficiently and effectively. Telling the truth is the best foundation for productive, long-term work relationships.

affecting them, you get a chance to see yourself as others see you, to understand their feelings and perceptions about you.

One of the best ways to understand the process of giving and receiving feedback was developed over 40 years ago by Joseph Luft and Harry Ingham. These two psychologists called their process the Johari Window. As shown in Fig. 6.1, the window they devised has four panes, each of which represents information you know about yourself and information others know about you.

The first pane, called the Open Area, includes things you know about yourself that others also know because you have shared

THE JOHARI WINDOW: A COMMUNICATION MODEL

	Things I Know	Things I Don't Know
Things Others Know	OPEN AREA	BLIND AREA
Things Others Don't Know	HIDDEN AREA	UNKNOWN AREA

Figure 6.1

information with them. You have made your ideas and feelings public; the information is out in the open. This area is characterized by a free and open exchange of ideas, and it increases in size as the level of mutual trust increases between you and others.

The second pane, called the Blind Area, includes things you do not know about yourself but others do because they have observed your behavior, listened to your tone of voice, or picked up nonverbal cues that you may not be aware of. This is sometimes called the bad-breath or in-the-dark area because you may not know how certain things about you—your style, behaviors, or mannerisms—are affecting others until they tell you. If you are not receptive to feedback from others, you may never know what kind of impression you are making on them.

The third pane, called the Hidden Area, includes information that you know about yourself but, for one reason or another, you do not share with others. In this area, there are things you know that you will not reveal until you feel the need to do so. This is sometimes called the facade area because people may put on a good face and intentionally withhold information to manipulate or control others. On the other hand, you may keep information from others because you feel sharing your opinions or perceptions might make them reject you or retaliate in some other negative way.

The fourth pane, called the Unknown Area, includes information that neither you nor others are aware of at first. When you suddenly

Danger!

- **Withholding data that could be helpful to others does not strengthen your position of power. It may, instead, send a message to others that you are petty, narrow-minded, and willing to get ahead at someone else's expense.**

become conscious of certain behaviors, motives, memories, or latent possibilities, you have what are often called "Aha! Experiences." You bring to the surface information that may have been so hidden or buried that neither you nor others knew about it.

The key to building trusting relationships is finding the best ways to modify your Open Area. In fact, Fig. 6.2 illustrates that there are only two options.

1. You can expand your Open Area (and reduce your Blind Area) by *requesting feedback* from others. You can learn about yourself by encouraging others to share their observations and knowledge about your behaviors.

2. You can expand your Open Area (and reduce your Hidden Area) by *giving feedback* to others. You can help others understand your values, beliefs, and reactions to what is happening in your work relationships by sharing your feelings, thoughts, perceptions, and opinions.

EXPANDING YOUR OPEN AREA

REQUEST FEEDBACK ——— (OPENNESS) ——→

	OPEN	BLIND
GIVE INFORMATION OR FEEDBACK		
(DISCLOSURE)	HIDDEN	UNKNOWN

Figure 6.2

THE JOHARI WINDOW AS A SELF-ASSESSMENT TOOL

If you have a large Blind Area in your relationship with a coworker, there are a lot of things you do not know about yourself or your job performance. The other person does know certain things that could help you. What questions would you ask to get useful feedback from this person?

Your Questions:

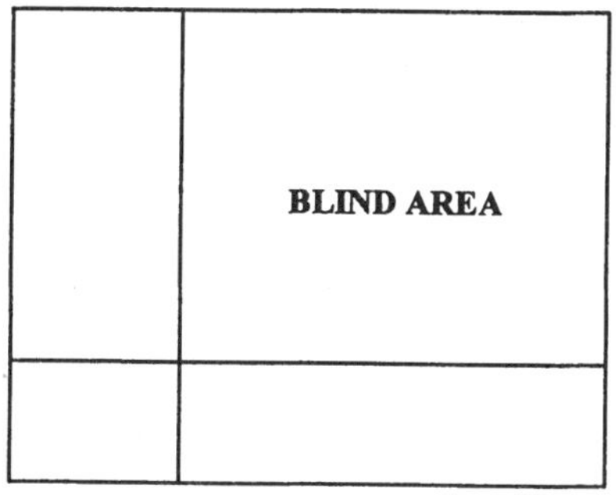

If you have a large Hidden Area in your relationship with a coworker, there are a lot of things you know about the other person and his or her job performance. The other person does not know certain things that could be helpful. What statements would you use to give useful feedback to this person?

Your Feedback:

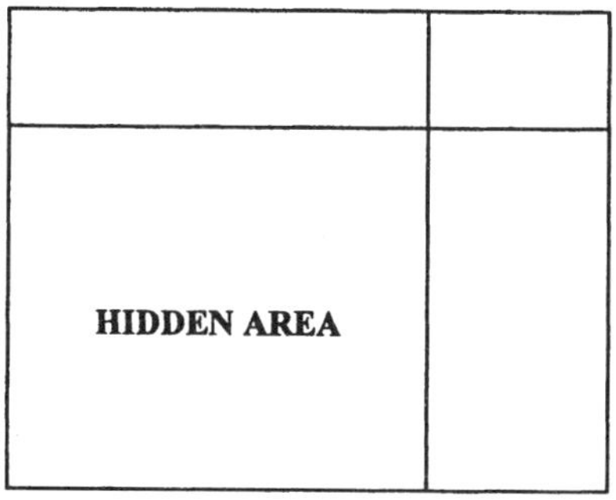

Figure 6.3

You may want to try using the Johari Window to plan a conversation with someone you work with. Use Fig. 6.3 to prepare questions you might ask someone with whom you have a large Blind Area or to prepare feedback you might give someone with whom you have a large Hidden Area.

Shortcut

• Learn about yourself by encouraging others to share their observations with you. Be receptive to their feedback. Do not get defensive or negative about what they have to say, or they will stop giving you information you may need. Get comfortable asking for performance-based feedback from all of your important constituents—your boss, coworkers, customers, and anyone else who can give you useful information about your work.

There are several key skills (highlighted in Fig. 6.4) that are essential whenever you are asking for feedback from others.

- Demonstrate that you are receptive to the information you have requested. Listen patiently to what the other person is saying, even though you may believe it is wrong or irrelevant. Indicate simple acceptance (not necessarily agreement) by nodding or injecting an occasional "um-hm" or "I see." Concentrate on the speaker's message. Stay focused. Try to understand both the content of the message and the other person's feelings about the message.

- Show interest. Listen carefully and attentively. Most people have difficulty talking clearly about their feelings, so paying careful attention is necessary. Listen also for what is *not* said. When people avoid key points or agree too quickly, these actions may be clues to something the person really wants to discuss but is uncomfortable doing. Body language, eye contact, tone of voice, and other cues might be part of the message being sent.

- Ask questions to make sure that you understand. Ask clarifying questions if you are not clear about the meaning of the message.

THE PROCESS OF SOLICITING INFORMATION OR FEEDBACK

RECEIVE THE INFORMATION
- Demonstrate receptivity.
- Listen carefully.
- Ask clarifying and probing questions.
- Resist justifying your behavior or becoming defensive.

INTERPRET THE INFORMATION
- Deal with personal biases and assumptions.
- Paraphrase and restate to make sure you understand.
- Reach agreement about the information.
- Confirm with others when possible.

Figure 6.4

Ask probing questions to learn more about the content or context of the message.

- Paraphrase or restate to make sure you have interpreted the information correctly. Confirm what you have heard by repeating or clarifying words, meanings, and feelings.

- Allow time for the discussion to continue without interruption. Focus on the content of the message. Try not to spend your listening time thinking about your next response. Reserve your evaluation of the other person's message until you are certain you understand it clearly. Do not make judgments until you have received all the information, then respond to the message received in a way that shows you have listened carefully.

- Reserve your evaluation or assessment of the message until you are certain you understand it clearly. Try not to make judgments until you know all the facts. If the person genuinely wants your viewpoint, be honest in your response. But in the listening process, try to limit expressing your views since these may affect how the other person responds. Remember what you should be most interested in is the other person's honest opinions, not a reflection of your own views. Reach agreement about what the other person's feedback means to you and to them.

Remember that the willingness to listen is one of the hallmarks of trusting communication.

Shortcut

- Help others understand your values, beliefs, and reactions to their performance by giving them honest, timely, accurate, and objective feedback. Be tactful and sensitive in your approach, but be certain also that you share information they need to improve their work and their relationship with you.

There are several key skills (highlighted in Fig. 6.5) that are essential whenever you are giving feedback to others.

- Test to see if the other person is receptive to your feedback. Select the best time, place, and approach. Use the right style, words, and tone.
- Be specific and clear. Focus on behavior (not the person), the specific (not generalizations), descriptions (not value judgments), and the person's immediate short-term need for feedback or information.
- Check to make sure the other person understands your feedback. Make sure the other person is not reading into your message, listening selectively, or hearing a different message from the one you are sending.
- Validate your feedback by using examples and other supporting information. Repeat the critical details to be sure your message has been received accurately. Summarize your feedback and ask for agreement about the message you have sent.

THE PROCESS OF GIVING INFORMATION OR FEEDBACK

TRANSMIT THE INFORMATION
- Establish receptivity.
- Be aware of your body language and nonverbal cues.
- Select the right style, words, and tone.
- Be specific and clear.
- Check for understanding.

VALIDATE THE INFORMATION
- Ask for or use examples.
- Summarize and ask for agreement.
- Clarify misunderstandings by restating or paraphrasing.
- Ask for and respond to questions.

Figure 6.5

In *Asserting Yourself: A Practical Guide for Positive Change* (Addison-Wesley, 1976), Sharon A. Bower and Gordon H. Bower developed a process for delivering difficult feedback to someone. Called the DESC Script, their approach is built on four sequential statements:

D escribe the behavior that is having a negative impact on you.
E xpress a feeling in response to that person's behavior.
S pecify the desired change you would like to see.
C larify consequences if the desired change does not occur.

Initially, the Bowers' model was used primarily in giving constructive or negative feedback in situations where the ongoing relationship was not important. Note how the tone in the following example might damage rather than strengthen the relationship:

1. *Describe the behavior* that is having a negative impact on you: "When you tell me you'll contact a customer about a shipping date and then don't follow through. . . ."

2. *Express a feeling* in response to that person's behavior: ". . . I feel angry."

3. *Specify the desired change* you would like to see: "I would prefer that you make good on your commitment. . . ."

4. *Clarify consequences* if the desired change does not occur: ". . . or I will look for someone else to work with me."

In recent years, however, the DESC Script has become a useful way to prepare and deliver a message about someone else's behavior. As the following examples demonstrate, the approach can work for either negative or positive feedback.

- *When you* give me negative feedback in front of others, *I* feel embarrassed, and *it makes me feel* intimidated. *I would prefer* that you talk to me in private *so that* our differences stay between us, and we can discuss them without interference from others.

- *When you* ask for my opinion about new procedures, *I* feel that you value my ideas and experience. *I would like it if you* keep me in mind for future discussions about these changes *because* I feel I can make a contribution that will be helpful to others in the group.

Don't Forget

- Your reputation will precede you, so make sure people are telling each other that you can be trusted to tell the truth.

In their book *Credibility,* James M. Kouzes and Barry Z. Posner describe being open to others as an important way to engender trust and establish credibility.

Trusting other people encourages them to trust us; distrusting others makes them lose confidence in us. We can help people trust us by the candor with which we talk about our behavior.

The authors also describe what can happen when there is a lack of trust.

You may know someone is clearly competent, dynamic, and inspirational. But if you have a sense that the person is not being honest, you will not accept the message, and you will not willingly follow. So the credibility check can reliably be simplified to just one question: "Do I trust this person?"

Effective communication is *primarily* the speaker's responsibility. When you are sending a message to someone else, be sure it is sent in an open, honest, and clear manner so that it does not require a great deal of decoding by the receiver. You need to be alert for any signs that the receiver may be confused or may have misunderstood your message. Finally, you need to be aware of the nonverbal aspects of communication (body language, gestures, eye contact, appearance, intonation, and facial expressions) to ensure that no mixed messages are being sent.

Effective communication also depends on the speaker's reputation, credibility, and intention. When you are the speaker, the person sending a message to someone else, the success of your communication will depend on how the other person answers these questions about you.

- Have you been clear, straightforward, honest, and trustworthy in the past?

- Can the person you are talking with believe you and your message?

- Does the other person believe the conversation is an attempt to manipulate, embarrass, or dominate him or her?

- Can the other person trust your motives or is there a possibility that you have a hidden agenda?

Danger!

- Hidden agendas keep others in the dark and create blind spots that damage relationships. If you mask your true intentions or hide your real feelings long enough, others will always wonder if they are hearing the truth from you or worry that they may not be able to completely trust your actions or your motives.

Lonnie Barone, president of Barone Associates, has been helping executives and professionals develop credibility for over 25 years. In his writings and presentations, he describes credibility as "the passive voice dimension" because "it exists not in you but in the person with whom you are credible."

Don't Forget

- You may never know that you have lost credibility with someone because they may not value your relationship enough to tell you. They may, however, tell everyone else.

According to Mr. Barone, credibility is based on four perceptions others have of you.

- *Honesty.* People think you tell them the truth.
- *Responsiveness.* People believe you come through for them. They believe you have access to the resources needed to make things happen, that you have the intelligence, the energy, and the ability to carry it off.
- *Trustworthiness.* People believe you are consistent and reliable. They believe that you can be depended on and that you are available to them. They believe you won't change your mind from one day to the next.

- *Forethought.* People think you make sense. They see the things you say as thoughtful, logical, and based on sound reasoning. You are not perceived as impulsive or rash. The things you say seem logical, based on sound supposition, resilient to critical examination.

In Mr. Barone's work with many successful organizations, there are important payoffs when you take the time to establish and maintain credibility. His experience confirms that:

- Honesty generates confidence. The perception of honesty means people believe you. Communication is clean, clear, efficient. Messages are taken at face value, not analyzed and reprocessed. People listen for content rather than motive.

- Responsiveness generates loyalty. If others think you come through for them, they will come through for you. If credibility is strong, this loyalty has real staying power. Others will stay with you in a crisis.

- Consistency and reliability generate trust. You are literally trustworthy. Others know you will not change course, reverse priorities, or lose enthusiasm. Others trust you and the course on which you have embarked. They do not fear sudden changes or unexpected priority shifts.

- Forethought generates respect. Others believe you give thought to the things you say and do. They respect you. Respect is really a sense of security. Others feel secure that you know what you are doing.

Mr. Barone is convinced that there are four qualities that allow you to build credibility with others.

First, there is knowledge. You know what you are talking about. You are an authority. You have done your homework. The second quality is competence. You have know-how. You are skilled at what you do. You deliver the goods because you *can* deliver the goods. The third quality is experience. You have been at it awhile, long enough to develop a track record and to develop knowledge and competence. If you are new at your job, you will lack credibility for a while, and you will have to earn it. The fourth quality is integrity. Simply put, integrity means that what you project on the outside is what you truly are inside. The person you portray is the person you are.

Shortcut

- Maintain your integrity even when you meet with resistance. The people who really count will respect your decision to stand by those beliefs that matter most to you, rather than changing chameleon style just to fit in when the environment seems to be different.

In his position as communication manager for a Fortune 500 organization, Steve Ozer believes that people need to be politically skillful in the most positive and honest sense of the word.

The reputation you develop over time is the most valuable thing you have. Office politics is a question of building and maintaining a reputation. Politics means that you sometimes have to make a choice between doing everything and doing the right thing. Saying no is one of the toughest things to do, but it is the most powerful way to build your reputation because you are saying yes to the right projects and the right people. That's really powerful! I've seen managers who have said yes to everything, and, over time, their reputation has eroded and they have gotten the label yes men or yes women. The ability to say no to someone, but then direct them to someone who can help, that's effective politics.

Joseph Toto remembers two specific incidents that reinforce for him the importance of telling the truth. Both occurred while he was managing a staff in a large pharmaceutical company:

One of the people reporting to me did not like a particular project assignment. I told her truthfully that another department really wanted her for the project and how hard it would be to get out of it or find someone else to do it. I told her exactly what was going on and reminded her that she was the person responsible. There was no getting away from it. After our meeting, she said I had been "refreshingly honest" and that she knew exactly where she stood as soon as I did. She went on to complete the project knowing she had my support and that of the department who had asked for her.

On another occasion, I learned an important lesson at the end of a major reengineering project. The project manager asked if we should emphasize the positives and downplay the negatives. My boss said that there was no need to "stack things artificially for our senior management." He said, "Let's tell the truth. People can learn from their mistakes and get better." There was no finger-pointing or blaming others. The report was honest, objective, and extremely useful. We all learned from it.

Telling the truth involves more than avoiding lies. It entails letting rumors that you cannot substantiate stop with you. It requires challenging water-cooler stories passed on to you as gospel so that you know what's absolutely true before you pass the tale on to someone else. It means knowing how to manage the office grapevine so that you are not caught in its tendrils.

In his book *Power! How to Get It, How to Use It* (Random House, 1975), Michael Korda provides a tongue-in-cheek perspective on a facet of office politics that is often misunderstood and misused:

Gossip has always come in for a bad press, and the person who is interested in power should certainly avoid gossiping to anyone. That does not mean it's a bad idea to *listen* to gossip. Quite the contrary: all gossip is worth hearing if you are strong enough to resist commenting on it, embellishing it, or passing it along. It pays to be a good listener, and to cultivate the habit of nodding wisely, as if you already knew about whatever you've been told. By carefully cultivating silence and reticence it is possible to build a valuable reputation as a person who knows a great deal and has probably been pledged to secrecy by some higher authority.

The old adage, honesty is the best policy, has significant political implications. In today's business world, honesty is the *only* policy.

Often it is not the easiest path, but it is always the right one. It is much better to build a reputation based on honesty than a career based on lies, empty promises, and deception. You will get much more satisfaction and respect in your organization if others know that they can trust your word. You will also sleep a lot better at night.

It's a Wrap

✔ You owe it to your company and to yourself to be the best you can possibly be. Regardless of the situation or the pressure to do otherwise, stay true to yourself. Be credible, trustworthy, and reliable at all costs. If, for some unfortunate reason, integrity is not valued in your current organization, perhaps it is time to find one of the many other companies around where being authentic is appreciated and rewarded.

✔ When communicating with others, use language that is clear, accurate, objective, and descriptive of events, actions, or behaviors that actually occurred.

✔ Share as much information as possible so that others perceive you as helpful, competent, confident, and willing to collaborate with them.

✔ Avoid changing your story to fit different situations. Telling lies requires a phenomenal memory and takes an incredible amount of counterproductive time and energy to avoid "the tangled webs we weave when once we practice to deceive." Telling the truth is easier, better, much more productive.

CHAPTER 7

POLITICAL TECHNIQUE 5
Be Professional in the Way You Look and Act

No matter how humble your work may seem, do it in the spirit of an artist, of a master. In this way, you lift it out of commonness and rob it of what would otherwise be drudgery.—**Orison Swett Marden**

If you're going to play the game properly, you'd better know every rule.—**Barbara Jordan**

Do I Need to Read This Chapter?

➡ Do you know exactly what it takes to be a professional in your organization?

➡ Are you familiar with all of your company's written standards?

➡ Do you know the unwritten rules people will use to judge your performance, appearance, and behavior?

Professionalism applies to the conduct of work activities and is a way of life in the best companies. Professionalism requires communication, commitment, accountability, teamwork, and mutual respect. In companies known for their professionalism, employees consistently demonstrate the following behaviors:

- Meet commitments with quality work
- Set and act according to high personal and professional standards
- Are organized and mentally ready to do the job
- Consider themselves part of a team that meets company objectives
- Take accountability for all aspects of their job
- Demonstrate pride of ownership for their work efforts
- Practice effective communication with all levels of the organization
- Treat coworkers with respect
- Work together to correct problems, resolve open issues, and ensure timely follow-up action
- Make the most of training and are continuous learners, responsible for improving their job skills
- Request and respond to feedback about ways to improve performance
- Examine work processes and take prompt corrective action to ensure or improve work quality
- Follow company and industry safety standards
- Are willing to change
- Conduct regular self-assessments and practice self-discipline
- Deal with issues on a professional (nonpersonal) level
- Maintain the big picture by understanding and respecting company values
- Foster teamwork in everyday work efforts
- Meet customer needs, both internally and externally

Quick Tips

Q: What does professionalism mean?

A: Professionalism means competence in what you do for a living and includes those procedures, standards, values, and common courtesies considered proper in dealing with people at work.

Q: How do you know what your company means by professionalism?

A: There are *written* and *unwritten* rules coworkers and managers expect you to observe and that you can expect from others. *Written* rules are the company policies and procedures that describe how business is done in your company. You are expected to conform to these established standards. *Unwritten* rules imply a choice of behavior. As you might expect, and as you may have experienced in dealing with others at work, the choices individuals make about their language, appearance, actions, and interactions influence your impression of them. Their choices may also affect your impressions of the department or organization for which they work and how you feel about dealing with them in the future.

Q: What happens when people are not professional in their performance or behavior?

A: When people's behaviors or work habits interfere with their job performance or the performance of others, they are less likely to succeed, and their colleagues are not likely to see them as a valued asset to the work group. The ultimate effect of an absence of professional standards is a demoralized organization or work group.

You are a true professional if you are:

- Competent and effective in delivering required results
- A comfortable person to meet and work with
- Appropriately dressed and neat in appearance and grooming
- Willing to collaborate with others by sharing information and expertise

Get Started

1. Learn your company's rules as quickly as you can. Talk to your supervisor. Observe people around you. Determine which behaviors are acceptable to your supervisor, your coworkers, and your constituents.

2. Identify factors that have helped or hindered other people in your company in the past. Try to understand how people have gotten ahead and how they have gotten in trouble with their superiors or peers.

3. Establish an honest, open relationship with your supervisor. Ask questions, seek advice, and listen carefully to suggestions about ways you can maintain your professionalism.

4. Build strong relationships with your coworkers by being open and friendly.

If you are a true professional, others can count on you to:

- Observe written policies, procedures, and safety rules
- Have a consistent attendance record
- Be ready to get down to business when the shift or work activity begins
- Return from lunch and breaks on time
- Get your own work accomplished accurately and on time
- Refrain from conducting personal business during work hours

Don't Forget

- Keep your business and personal life separate. Try not to let home matters interfere with your work.

If you are a true professional, people trust and respect you because you:

- Are fair and patient with everyone
- Keep commitments
- Respect confidentiality and do not spread rumors or betray personal confidences
- Do not badmouth or criticize people
- Will not compromise your own personal standards
- Try to understand others' problems and pressures
- Are a problem solver

You earn the respect of others by treating them in a professional way: by showing courtesy, competence, and confidence. Your most challenging interactions with certain people are those in which you feel they lack respect for you and your abilities. Sometimes this lack of respect is unfair and unfounded. You may be treated inappropriately by people who do not know you or who do not give you a chance to demonstrate your skills. Often their approach is not intentional or malicious. They may be so caught up in their own problems that they don't realize how they are treating you. People who act aggressively may really be worried; a person who has a know-it-all attitude may really be embarrassed or confused.

For whatever reasons, however, when you are not treated with respect, you need to do the best you can do to take charge of the situation and not let it overwhelm or discourage you. In other words, you need to maintain your self-esteem and handle the situation as professionally as you can. Two techniques can be helpful in these difficult situations:

1. Show empathy by recognizing and acknowledging the feelings of others. This approach:

   - Lets people know you are concerned and want to help them
   - Diffuses the emotion in a conversation and lets you focus on problems and solutions

- Allows you to reach common understanding with others (although you may not agree with their feelings) so that you can identify and address the causes of these feelings

- Demonstrates patience and your willingness to go that extra mile for others.

2. Be factual about your own feelings in a way that shows you are in control of yourself and the situation. This approach:

- Lets others know you can be assertive (not aggressive) and persuasive (not pushy) in the way you do your job

- Helps to reestablish your role in the conversation so that you are not manipulated or forced to make unacceptable concessions

- Clarifies your feelings with people who may not be showing you the same degree of understanding or concern you have shown them

- Lets you clear the air concisely and diplomatically so that you can focus again on facts (not feelings) and outcomes (not emotions)

Don't Forget

- Be authentic. People need to feel they can trust you, that you will tell them the truth, that you will be fair and reliable. If you genuinely care about others, they will know it, sense it, and respond to you in a positive way. If you lie to someone, you immediately damage your credibility with that person and anyone else he or she decides to talk to about you. In some cases, you may never know how badly you have damaged your reputation because people won't care enough to take the time to tell you.

If you are a true professional, you will have credibility with others because you do the following.

- Keep control of your temper and emotions
- Admit mistakes and do not try to shift blame to others
- Do not pretend to know all the answers
- Help others to learn
- Look for opportunities to help others succeed
- Respect individual differences

Take a few minutes to complete the self-assessment questionnaire in Fig. 7.1 to determine your current level of professionalism and to determine areas you may want to improve.

Danger!

- Don't tell jokes or stories that will offend others. Be sensitive to individual and cultural differences between you and your coworkers. What may seem acceptable to you may not be to others, so think before you do or say something that may be offensive.

In some organizations, there may be real, perceived, or potential conflicts between:

- What is *really* the right thing to do and what people feel they have a right to do
- Universal or commonly shared values and individual or personal preferences

Shortcut

- Talk to your supervisor about the difference between acceptable and excellent performance. Find out what level of productivity you need to achieve now and what level you will need to reach in the near future.

PERSONAL ASSESSMENT

Read each of the descriptors listed below and rate your own level of professionalism. Based on your personal assessment, check off the areas you plan to improve.

Others would say you are:	Needs Work	Good	Exemplary
A comfortable person to meet.	❏	❏	❏
Neat in appearance and grooming.	❏	❏	❏
Appropriately dressed.	❏	❏	❏
Others feel they can count on you because you:			
Observe written policies, procedures, and safety rules.	❏	❏	❏
Have a consistent attendance record.	❏	❏	❏
Are ready to go when your shift or work activity begins.	❏	❏	❏
Return from breaks and lunch on time.	❏	❏	❏
Get your own work accomplished accurately and on time.	❏	❏	❏
Don't conduct personal business during work hours.	❏	❏	❏
People trust and respect you because you:			
Are fair and patient with everyone.	❏	❏	❏
Keep commitments.	❏	❏	❏
Respect confidentiality and don't spread rumors.	❏	❏	❏
Don't badmouth or criticize people.	❏	❏	❏
Don't compromise personal standards just to fit in.	❏	❏	❏
Try to understand others' problems and pressures.	❏	❏	❏
Are a problem solver.	❏	❏	❏
You have integrity & credibility with others because you:			
Keep control of your temper and emotions.	❏	❏	❏
Admit mistakes and don't try to shift blame.	❏	❏	❏
Don't pretend to know all the answers.	❏	❏	❏
Help others learn.	❏	❏	❏
Look for opportunities to help others succeed.	❏	❏	❏
Respect individual differences.	❏	❏	❏

Figure 7.1

- What people *really* deserve or have earned and what they feel they are entitled to

If there are questionable preferences or practices in your company, try to do everything you can do to remove potential obstacles to your productivity and professionalism. If you are uncertain about what is expected of you, ask your immediate supervisor to clarify any of the following items:

- *Your job responsibilities, duties, and performance standards.* Ask your supervisor to state in specific terms what quantity and quality of work he or she expects from you. If you have certain time commitments and cost restraints, make sure you understand them clearly.

- *Behavioral guidelines.* Ask your supervisor to discuss any cautions about acceptable or unacceptable behavior in the way you do your job. For example, many companies today put a high value on teamwork and effective interpersonal relationships. If this is true in your company, you will want to know so that you can act accordingly.

- *Company policies.* Ask your supervisor to answer any questions you have about smoking, dress code, time off, overtime, benefit programs, and work schedules. Remember that most companies have both written and unwritten rules, so you may want to focus on how things are really done here.

Don't Forget

- Dress in a manner that does not distract others or keep them or you from being productive and professional.

- *Departmental procedures.* Ask your supervisor to discuss day-to-day operations (like schedules, routine work problems, and customer complaints) and special situations (like family emergencies, personal or sick leave, and equipment breakdowns). Take the time to find out how your supervisor would like you to handle minor problems, major crises, and your work relationship with each other. Find out how your supervisor would like to be kept informed about your work. Will your supervisor expect written reports, regular meetings, routine observations, informal verbal updates, or a combination of these and other techniques?

- *Where to get help.*   Ask your supervisor to name the resources you can go to when you need help and he or she is not around. This list should include the person you can go to for permission or authority to do something out of the ordinary and anyone else outside your department who has special expertise that might be useful to you in an emergency.

- *Land mines and red alerts.*   Ask your supervisor to discuss potential problems and how to solve, resolve, or avoid them. Find out what your supervisor wants you to do when you encounter these barriers or obstacles. You may be expected to deal with a customer's complaint one way and a complaint from another department in a different way, so make sure you clarify how your supervisor wants you to handle specific situations.

In general, there are several social taboos that are unacceptable in any company at any time. If you are sensitive to people, you will probably automatically be politically correct and appropriate in your dealings with them. Here are some cardinal rules to remember:

- Do not use language that offends, belittles, or demeans any group or individual. Use bias-free, nondiscriminatory language that stays clear of sexist or racist comments and avoids any put-downs based on a person's nationality, age, academic background, work experience, or job title. We all have biases and prejudices that can lead to stereotypes and other unfair expectations or reactions. The first step in dealing with these biases is to understand what they are. If you find yourself making generalizations like "All young people are only interested in getting ahead at the expense of others" or "All engineers are too detail-oriented to be concerned about the people on their work teams," you have strong biases that could interfere with your work performance if you do not take care to monitor your language and your behavior. One insensitive comment or rude action can have a powerful negative impact on your relationship with one or many individuals.

- Show respect for others—their time, their space, their priorities. Unless there is an emergency, try not to impose on others or interrupt them with problems that should be discussed by appointment. Even if executives boast about their open-door policy, do not presume to drop in casually for something that may be perceived as unimportant or low priority. Schedule time with managers and be sure they know the nature, scope, and importance of your agenda. Casual, small-talk meetings are appropriate if you keep them short and know when to let the other person get on with business. Remember, there may be a better time and place to discuss what's important to you, especially if the other person seems absorbed, distracted, or energized by something else. If someone shows disrespect for your time, space, and priorities, it is your responsibility to confront the issue and suggest a better alternative like: "Can we talk about this over lunch because I'm trying to finish this report right now" or "How about if I come to your office later this morning after I've responded to this customer's inquiry?"

- Don't criticize others or their ideas in public. Be especially careful about negative feelings you have about your supervisor or other managers. Get to know the people you can talk to privately about your concerns and focus your efforts on the constructive resolution of these problems. Always consider a face-to-face discussion with the person you are critical of as your first course of action. If that fails, you may want to resort to getting help, in a positive way, from your immediate supervisor or someone with the authority and the right intentions to assist or support you.

Don't Forget

- Your organization has its own culture developed over the years by employees who have done things in a particular way. If you are unfamiliar with those customs or unwritten rules, you need to observe how people work with each other and determine what behaviors are acceptable. Don't compromise your own professional standards, but be aware that you may need to adapt your style or change some of your preferences to be effective in your company's unique culture.

One aspect of professionalism that has received renewed interest recently is the area that used to be called dress for success. Today, many organizations have instituted casual Fridays or relaxed their standards for certain employees in certain situations. For some companies there are no written dress code policies—expectations are communicated informally and verbally. For other companies, because casual has been taken to an unacceptable extreme, written rules have been developed to define professional dress and appearance, usually from the perspective of what customers have a right to expect from their service providers.

When the rules are not specific or explicit, sometimes it helps to get help from someone who has had practical experience with company guidelines and practices. For one executive we know, it was friendly advice from a coworker that a corduroy sport coat was not appropriate in the three-piece business suit work environment he had recently joined. For Rosemary Adiletto, prevention program coordinator at a nonprofit organization, the unwritten rule leaned more toward casual clothing:

Work clothes became important. I needed to dress and act according to new ways. In my new organization, anything goes. It's hard to tell the staff from the clients. I tried to appeal to their sense of how we needed to appear to the public. But, in the end, I changed to fit their culture. The norms have changed. I tell people who do training programs with me to dress one step up from their audience. People still disagree with this but it's as far as I'm willing to go. In general, I think your success on the job depends on how much you are willing to change to meet your company's norms.

I also think the advantages of age are underestimated by today's workers. Credibility comes with experience. People respond to someone's ability to grow old and change with the times. People admire and respect that.

The ability to change with the times without compromising your own standards is both advisable and difficult. Most of us have deep-seated principles that govern our behavior and dictate how we treat other people. There are commonly held values—like honesty, respect for others, fairness, being considerate—that most people embrace and practice. Peter Block points out that our professional standards are often rooted in strong personal beliefs about how we should deal with others:

> It is in our self-interest to treat other people well. All of us care deeply about the well-being of our colleagues and the people around us. Organizations for most of us are the primary meeting place. We each have strong personal values and often religious values about how other people are to be treated.

Treating others well, then, is an important attribute that identifies you as someone with high professional standards and a strong commitment to the well-being of others. Caring about people is one of the cornerstones of positive political behavior. There are, of course, some specific challenges that may test your commitment to these principles. There is always the possibility that you will meet somebody who will want you to bend the rules too often and too far, compromise your integrity for personal gain, or participate in activities that are counterproductive. You may be faced with occasional temptations to ignore the golden rule. It is important to take frequent self-assessments to ensure that you are maintaining your own high personal standards. Your good reputation depends on it.

For example, if your job gives you access to confidential or proprietary information, remember to keep it to yourself. It is essential to be known as a person who is trustworthy and dependable, someone who can be counted on to be diplomatic and discreet. Spreading bad news, rehashing every mistake the company has made, and taking wild guesses about new strategies or approaches wastes a lot of time and can demoralize the people around you.

Maintain a positive perspective and don't let yourself be hooked into these doom and gloom conversations. Although complaining is a common practice in most work settings, there is no reason why you have to take part in this counterproductive activity. If there is a problem with another person or department, get it resolved and get on with your work. You will feel much better getting results than getting a reputation as a chronic complainer.

Sometimes being professional is more difficult than other times. Katherine Huston remembers a particular challenge:

> I had been told that my job would be eliminated within the next three months. Despite this, my company expected me to continue doing training programs as though that wasn't happening to me. The irony was, I was conducting workshops on career development and retirement planning. Trainees would come up to me and say, "We heard a rumor that you're losing your job, but we knew it couldn't be true because you wouldn't have been able to be so calm and so professional in class." It was important for me to be professional and continue to do my job well. I knew I could not let people down who depended on me.

Danger!

- Avoid back-stabbing, name-calling, finger-pointing, or other underhanded practices. Avoid the rumor mill. Develop social savvy about what you can do or say in the presence of coworkers.

To maintain your professionalism, learn not to burn bridges. Look instead for opportunities to build them by developing meaningful relationships with superiors and peers. Although your upward relationships are important and need to be developed and sustained, peer relationships also need to be recognized and nurtured. You must establish a strong network of contacts who are willing to keep you informed about any conditions or activities that will have an immediate impact on your performance. You may want to ask your supervisor to take a few minutes to complete the questionnaire in Fig. 7.2 to help you determine your current level of professionalism and to determine areas you may want to improve.

Shortcuts

- Read everything you can about your company's history, products, services, policies, procedures, and financial position. Ask questions about anything you do not understand. Learn about company benefits, training opportunities, and career development resources.

Peer relationships can influence your job satisfaction, your ability to achieve desired results, and make or break your career. You may want to ask one of your coworkers to take a few minutes to complete the questionnaire in Fig. 7.3 to help you determine your current level of professionalism and to identify areas you may want to improve. Friendly colleagues can often provide you with information, resources, and support to help you meet deadlines, produce quality outcomes, and launch or complete important projects. On the other hand, hostile or disgruntled peers can create conflict, put obstacles in your path, or drag their feet to make you look bad in front of others.

Always be courteous and diplomatic. If you do not know basic business etiquette, take the time to learn the business manners that are acceptable in your company. Observe how key managers and

SUPERVISOR'S ASSESSMENT

Ask your supervisor to rate you on each of the descriptors listed below. Based on your supervisor's assessment of your professionalism, check off the areas you plan to improve.

Others would say you are:	Needs Work	Good	Exemplary
A comfortable person to meet.	❑	❑	❑
Neat in appearance and grooming.	❑	❑	❑
Appropriately dressed.	❑	❑	❑
Others feel they can count on you because you:			
Observe written policies, procedures, and safety rules.	❑	❑	❑
Have a consistent attendance record.	❑	❑	❑
Are ready to go when your shift or work activity begins.	❑	❑	❑
Return from breaks and lunch on time.	❑	❑	❑
Get your own work accomplished accurately and on time.	❑	❑	❑
Don't conduct personal business during work hours.	❑	❑	❑
People trust and respect you because you:			
Are fair and patient with everyone.	❑	❑	❑
Keep commitments.	❑	❑	❑
Respect confidentiality and don't spread rumors.	❑	❑	❑
Don't badmouth or criticize people.	❑	❑	❑
Don't compromise personal standards just to fit in.	❑	❑	❑
Try to understand others' problems and pressures.	❑	❑	❑
Are a problem solver.	❑	❑	❑
You have integrity & credibility with others because you:			
Keep control of your temper and emotions.	❑	❑	❑
Admit mistakes and don't try to shift blame.	❑	❑	❑
Don't pretend to know all the answers.	❑	❑	❑
Help others learn.	❑	❑	❑
Look for opportunities to help others succeed.	❑	❑	❑
Respect individual differences.	❑	❑	❑

Figure 7.2

COWORKER'S ASSESSMENT

Ask one of your coworkers to read each of the descriptors listed below and rate your level of professionalism. Based on this feedback, check off the areas you plan to improve.

Others would say you are:	Needs Work	Good	Exemplary
A comfortable person to meet.	❏	❏	❏
Neat in appearance and grooming.	❏	❏	❏
Appropriately dressed.	❏	❏	❏
Others feel they can count on you because you:			
Observe written policies, procedures, and safety rules.	❏	❏	❏
Have a consistent attendance record.	❏	❏	❏
Are ready to go when your shift or work activity begins.	❏	❏	❏
Return from breaks and lunch on time.	❏	❏	❏
Get your own work accomplished accurately and on time.	❏	❏	❏
Don't conduct personal business during work hours.	❏	❏	❏
People trust and respect you because you:			
Are fair and patient with everyone.	❏	❏	❏
Keep commitments.	❏	❏	❏
Respect confidentiality and don't spread rumors.	❏	❏	❏
Don't badmouth or criticize people.	❏	❏	❏
Don't compromise personal standards just to fit in.	❏	❏	❏
Try to understand others' problems and pressures.	❏	❏	❏
Are a problem solver.	❏	❏	❏
You have integrity & credibility with others because you:			
Keep control of your temper and emotions.	❏	❏	❏
Admit mistakes and don't try to shift blame.	❏	❏	❏
Don't pretend to know all the answers.	❏	❏	❏
Help others learn.	❏	❏	❏
Look for opportunities to help others succeed.	❏	❏	❏
Respect individual differences.	❏	❏	❏

Figure 7.3

high potential employees deal with specific social or interpersonal situations. For example, you may want to notice:

- How they say no diplomatically so that others do not interpret their resistance as negative, uncooperative, or unwilling to be flexible
- How they dress for certain meetings or occasions
- What they eat and drink (or do not eat or drink) at business luncheons or power breakfasts and when they actually get down to talking business during these social/work meetings
- How much time they spend listening to others and how they respond when they hear bad news or when their ideas meet with resistance or opposition

There are several other common courtesies you may want to remember and practice:

- Return phone calls and respond to e-mail messages as quickly as possible. Although you may not have time right now to go into detail about a specific question or concern, acknowledging that you have received the other person's message is a simple but important business courtesy. Saying "Thanks for your call. Can we talk later this week?" lets others know that they are important to you and that you will make time to respond to them again soon.
- Arrive for meetings on time. Coming late for meetings was once a popular power play people would use to prove how important they were to others waiting for a meeting to start. Now, lateness is usually regarded as an inconsiderate waste of time and productivity. If you show up 10 minutes late for a meeting that involves six other people, you have effectively cost your company one hour of productive work time. The later you are or the larger the meeting group, the greater the time lost and the aggravation you cause among your coworkers. Keep an accurate, updated calendar so that you do not keep people waiting because you forgot, double-booked yourself, or underestimated the time it would

take for you to finish a task preceding your next appointment. If you cannot help yourself, and know you will be late, let others know as soon as possible. Just showing up late is inconsiderate and will probably be disruptive.

- Answer correspondence as soon as you can, especially if it comes from one of your customers. If you neglect this common courtesy, many of your external customers will go over your head and send a follow-up letter to someone at the top of your organization. These second-chance letters will often mention you by name as the person who failed to give satisfactory service the first time. Your internal customers may be less likely to complain to someone higher in the chain of command. But your failure to respond to one of their memos has been documented and probably filed away for future use. This CYA (cover your anatomy) behavior is typical in situations where there is competition for resources or pressure to complete a project that has unrealistic expectations. Know which customers can cause you the greatest harm and put their correspondence at the top of your stack.

- Send a personal message to any coworker who would welcome hearing from you. We have a colleague who leaves brief e-mail messages such as "Welcome back. Hope you're feeling better!" and "Glad you got the promotion. You worked hard for it." whenever something noteworthy happens in her department. A brief visit, note, or telephone call that is not entirely business-related lets others know you are interested in them as people and not just work associates. As long as they are not intrusive, personal exchanges like these can foster teamwork with your peers. They can also help you establish the foundation for a stronger relationship that can allow you to offer your support to others when there are professional setbacks or personal crises.

Your peer relationships are built on countless daily contacts, from informal greetings on the morning elevator ride to formal exchanges during a project team meeting. Although the spontaneous, informal exchanges are more common, they are often on the spur of the moment, and you may miss an opportunity to create a stronger connection with some of your peers. In some cases, a simple greeting can set the stage for a more meaningful connection. For example, you can enhance your relationships with peers by doing the following.

- Asking for advice: "How does your group handle irate customers?"
- Asking for an update: "How's the Magellan project going?"
- Discussing a problem: "How will downsizing in the marketing department affect your project?"

In other cases, these informal contacts can be useful to establish a more formal relationship usually characterized by scheduling a meeting or a more in-depth discussion of something that has mutual interest or benefit. Establishing good relationships with your peers can expedite processes, give you a different perspective on important problems, gain support of current or future projects, and provide evidence to your manager that cooperation and teamwork are important to you. All of these behaviors are evidence that you are a true professional in the way you approach your job.

It's a Wrap

✔ The individual choices you make about your language, appearance, actions, and relationships with others at work will influence their impression of you. If you want to be known as a true professional, it is your responsibility to understand the written and unwritten rules your company has about work standards and performance expectations.

✔ Respect the people you work with and expect the same from them. Most of us want to do a good job and want to work in a comfortable, harmonious environment. It is in your own self-interest to be helpful, courteous, and cordial to others. Being considerate usually generates a positive response and can strengthen work relationships.

CHAPTER 8

POLITICAL TECHNIQUE 6
Choose Your Battles Strategically

Pick battles big enough to matter, small enough to win.
—Jonathan Kozol

There's nothing more awkward than a misunderstanding left unresolved. And nothing more unnecessary. It leads to strain, tension, invective, an atmosphere that can lead to open hostility. Why risk losing a friend, a colleague, a customer? If you have a misunderstanding that is a tempest in a teapot, don't let it blow into a hurricane. Take the initiative. Pick up the phone. Pick up a pen. Or pick yourself up. March in right now and clear the air.—**Message as published in the** *Wall Street Journal* **by United Technologies Corporation, Hartford, Connecticut**

Do I Need to Read This Chapter?

→ How effective are you at resolving interpersonal conflicts with coworkers and superiors?

→ How effective are you at confronting difficult people?

→ How do you deal with people who enjoy power plays and use game playing to get what they want?

Most organizational activities depend on successful networking, negotiating, and problem solving. Finding mutually acceptable solutions to difficult problems and resolving conflicts effectively require political behaviors and actions that depend on your ability to influence the right people. Power differences among individuals who interact with each other and attempt to influence each other in different ways can increase the probability of conflict about goals, priorities, resources, and methodologies.

Conflict is inevitable; in fact, it is usually necessary if you want to move an idea or any activity forward. There will always be resistance, differences of opinion, diverse perspectives about how, when, and why to proceed. In and of itself, conflict is not negative, problematic, disruptive, or counterproductive. It is a natural occurrence that must be recognized and managed effectively so that it enhances cooperation and teamwork rather than creating unhealthy tension or unnecessary antagonism.

Conflict begins when the conditions for a disagreement or competition exist. Individuals may have different goals or priorities, compete for scarce resources, view their roles differently, or feel conflicting work pressures. These differences provide the foundation for conflict which might, at first, be perceived but quickly ignored or denied. Once one person feels tense, anxious, or angry, the conflict becomes felt and personalized. Individuals take their appropriate sides in opposition to each other. Open antagonism and withdrawal of cooperation indicate that a real conflict is taking place.

Conflict occurs when mutually exclusive goals, values, or priorities exist or are perceived to exist by the people in conflict with each other. The individuals resort to behaviors that are intended to defeat, embarrass, or dominate the other side so that one person or group wins and the other loses something—face, status, credibility, or even a job. At this time, the conflict must be resolved or managed constructively so that individual, team, and organizational performance can be maintained. Figure 8.1 highlights some of the benefits of managing conflict effectively.

BENEFITS OF EFFECTIVE CONFLICT MANAGEMENT:

- There are high levels of communication.
- Collaboration, sharing, and supportive behaviors are practiced.
- Feedback is solicited and given freely.
- High levels of trust and respect exist.
- Tension and stress are minimized.
- Individual contributions are valued, recognized, and rewarded.
- People are allowed to be wrong.
- There are high levels of satisfaction, motivation, and morale.
- Productivity, effectiveness, and efficiency are enhanced.

Figure 8.1

Get Started

Here are some action steps to help you prepare to resolve an interpersonal conflict:

1. Describe the conflict as briefly and as specifically as possible: With whom? How long? What caused it? Has it gotten better or worse?

2. Describe the impact the conflict is having on your ability to achieve your work goals: quantity, quality, time, and costs.

3. Describe any broader impact you know this conflict is having on others in your work area, on your future relationships with this individual, on your overall level of trust and respect for this person.

4. Describe the benefits of resolving this conflict: to you, to the other person, to others.

Conflict expert Dr. Kenneth Thomas believes each conflict moves through four stages.

1. *Frustration.*   An individual or group cannot accomplish a goal or complete a task.
2. *Conceptualization.*   The individuals involved perceive that conflict exists and formulate ideas about the issue. They frequently gather information and consider multiple points of view to gain a better understanding of the issue.
3. *Behavior.*   Those affected respond to the conflict.
4. *Outcome.*   The conflict is resolved, or frustration continues and leads to another conflict episode.

According to Dr. Thomas, conflict can have both positive and negative consequences. If managed effectively, it can encourage innovation, creativity, and flexibility. Conflict can have several positive outcomes.

- More and better ideas
- A tendency to search for alternative approaches
- Resolution of old issues and problems
- Improved creativity and innovation
- Greater involvement in problem solving, ownership, commitment to solutions
- Opportunities to clarify personal interests, values, and expectations

Figure 8.2 highlights some of the other potentially positive outcomes that can be realized when conflict is managed or resolved effectively.

The benefits of dealing with conflict include:

- Stronger relationships
- Increased self-respect
- Personal development and growth

THE POSITIVE OUTCOMES OF CONFLICT

- A search for new information, solutions, or approaches is encouraged.
- Important problems, issues, and concerns are brought to the surface.
- Interpersonal, team, and organizational effectiveness is improved.
- Higher levels of communication, cooperation, and innovation are created and maintained.
- The process can lead to synergy and the generation of other possibilities beyond the two options originally proposed by the conflicting parties.

Figure 8.2

If conflict is not handled effectively, it can:

- Reduce productivity
- Cause dissatisfaction and lower morale
- Increase stress, tension, and suspicion among workers
- Produce a variety of other dysfunctional consequences

Figure 8.3 highlights some of the potentially negative outcomes that can occur when conflict is not managed or resolved effectively.

If conflict is seen as detrimental or potentially harmful, people avoid dealing with it and negative outcomes often occur.

- The situation gets worse; the gap between people increases.
- Someone loses, gets defeated, or gets the worst of the situation.
- A climate of mistrust, suspicion, or hostility is created.
- There is resistance and retaliation rather than harmony and teamwork.

THE NEGATIVE OUTCOMES OF CONFLICT

- Growing resentment sometimes hidden from others.
- Venting leads to badmouthing others behind their backs.
- Resistance to procedures, goals, or processes.
- Continued lack of cooperation on future projects or in subsequent discussions.
- Pushes people farther apart.
- Creates a climate of distrust and suspicion.
- Feeling of defeat reinforces avoidance behaviors.
- Higher levels of tension and stress exist.
- Time and energy are wasted on nonproductive behaviors and activities.

Figure 8.3

- Other coworkers, friends, and colleagues are dragged into the conflict to support each opposing side.
- Some temporary watered-down option gets suggested and adopted.

Quick Tips

Q: Why should I get involved trying to resolve a conflict I am having with someone at work?

A: Some people say, "I'm not getting paid to stick my neck out and deal with those kinds of problems" or "That's my supervisor's job, not mine." The only caution about letting someone else resolve your conflicts is that you may get a solution that you do not like or want. It is always much better to represent yourself, to provide your side of the disagreement, to present information as factually and objectively as possible, and hope that the other person listens and responds fairly. If not, then you may want to ask for a referee or arbiter to help the two of you reach an acceptable solution.

Q: What do I do if I cannot trust the person I am having a conflict with?

A: This is a very difficult situation. The best you can do is make an honest assessment about why you do not trust the other person, when your distrust began, and what the other person said or did to damage his or her credibility. If possible, try to discuss the issue of trust with the individual involved. There is a possibility the other person does not know the nature or extent of the problem. If you have already had this discussion or honestly believe it will not help, you probably will need to find someone you trust (your supervisor, another manager, a veteran coworker, an objective executive, or someone from your human resource area) to help you address both the conflict situation and the more sensitive issue of lost trust.

Dr. Thomas defines conflict as the process which begins when we perceive that someone has negatively affected or is about to negatively affect, something we care about. The more deeply we care about something, the more intense the conflict. As shown in Fig. 8.4, the positions people take when dealing with conflict are defined by how much they try to satisfy their own concerns (assertiveness) and how much they try to satisfy the other person's concerns (cooperation). Dr. Thomas describes five individual strategies for dealing with conflict.

1. *Avoidance* is a strategy in which an individual tries to resolve a conflict by withdrawing or by denying that a problem exists. This style is used when we believe everything will be better if we don't confront the issue or when we believe things will get worse if we discuss the problem. It is often called a lose-lose approach. Avoiding is the position where we are the most unassertive and the most uncooperative. Here, we attempt to satisfy neither our own concerns nor the concerns of the other party. In other words, our position is not to

THOMAS-KILMAN CONFLICT STYLES

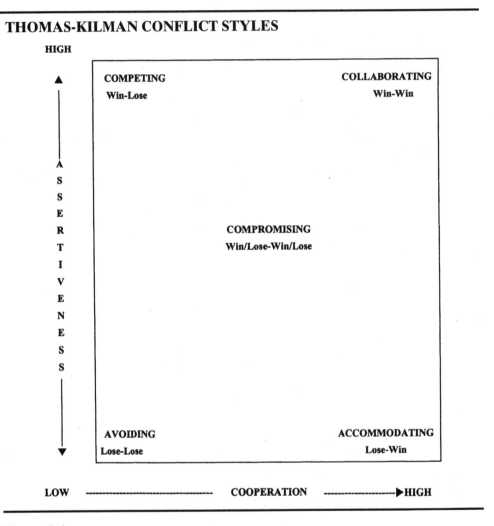

Figure 8.4

take a position, and the result is a stalemate where frustration and anger can build. Avoiding a conflict can be useful, particularly in situations where we feel the conflict is trivial or where we know we have no chance of satisfying our concerns, but many people prefer this approach in all of their work-related conflicts.

2. *Accommodation* is a strategy in which differences are minimized, smoothed over, or suppressed. Surface harmony is maintained, at least temporarily, because one individual goes along with whatever the other individual thinks is best. It is often called a lose-win approach. In taking an accommodating position during a conflict, we are making an attempt to satisfy concerns—only they are the concerns of the other party. When we accommodate the other party, we are being highly cooperative but unassertive. However, smoothing over a dispute can minimize our own needs and, in the end, make us feel powerless and frustrated. That action can inadvertently intensify the situation, upping the ante. Still, there are times when we may choose to accommodate the other party for a larger purpose, for example, to maintain harmony and stability in our organization.

3. *Competition* is a strategy which focuses on defeating or outshining another person rather than resolving the problem. In this type of adversarial contest, we may present an overwhelming amount of proof that our way is the best or only solution. It is often called a win-lose approach. Competing is the direct opposite of accommodating. When we compete, we are attempting to satisfy our own concerns while showing little interest in the needs of the other party. In fact, we are operating at the point of extreme lack of cooperation and high assertiveness. This classic conflict situation can make it appear to the warring parties that there is no solution in sight. Yet, while competing might seem to be a poor choice, it can be viable. There's no time, for instance, to address the other party's concerns in an emergency or when we are enforcing rules. Constructive conflict, where we encourage people to disagree and play devil's advocate, is different from competing to win at all costs. For those who believe that competition in general naturally fosters better performance, consultant Alfie Kohn offers the conclusion that "competition generally does not promote excellence because trying to do well and trying to beat others are simply two different things."

4. *Compromise* is a strategy in which each individual gives up something in order to meet in the middle. We make trade-offs to arrive at satisfactory outcomes and to save time. This type of negotiated settlement, based on mutual concessions, can reduce conflict without actually resolving it. It is often called a win/lose-win/lose approach. Many of us think of compromising as a natural conflict resolution technique. And actually, it can be partially effective in that way. As the position midway between competing and accommodating, compromise means we give up half of our concerns in order to get the other half. This is also known as splitting the difference or sharing. When we compromise, we behave in a moderately assertive and moderately cooperative fashion. Compromising can provide a workable solution in several situations: when we are operating under a deadline, when goals are likely to remain incompatible, or when the issues are too complex to be addressed in a timely manner.

5. *Collaboration* is a strategy which focuses on resolving the conflict. The experience, expertise, and perceptions of both parties are recognized and valued. Alternatives are discussed openly and decisions are made in a broader context: what is best for the team, the department, or the company. This approach often depends on using objective criteria to evaluate multiple options and solutions. It is often called a win-win approach. Collaborating is the most ideal position and the one that takes the most patience and commitment to achieve. Unlike accommodating, competing, and compromising, which only partially satisfy concerns, collaborating satisfies the concerns of all parties. When we take a collaborative position, we are being both highly assertive and highly cooperative. Collaborating is of particular use when we want to work through feelings to improve a relationship, when concerns are too important to be compromised or accommodated away, and when we are looking to build consensus.

If you want to accomplish more than you ever thought possible, remember it is easier to work *with* people than it is to work *against* them. Think of the hours of time and energy you (or people you know) have wasted on unnecessary disagreements or needless conflicts. The way you deal with conflict determines whether it has a positive and productive effect on your lives. By avoiding certain conflict situations, you may actually be harming yourself and the other person involved, especially if you waste time complaining about the problem (without resolving it) or working around other people (instead of working with them).

Johanna Zitto has worked in a variety of corporate settings before starting her own company. She believes conflict can sometimes emphasize gender differences.

> Some women approach a problem as a cause. They deliver ultimatums and take a selfish, rigid position. They view the problem as a battle to be won. I learned that a rational problem-solving approach was better than a zealous, radical approach. I try to stay focused on the issues, identify possible contributing factors, and then determine possible courses of action that can benefit all parties in some way.

Rosemary Stasak, a retail manager, describes the nature of occasional conflict with her superior.

> Sometimes my boss and I disagree about priorities. He wants me working on one thing when I know for sure our customers want something else first. These occasional conflicts can really cause problems for us. I actually wind up avoiding him so that he does not know I'm not doing exactly what he wants me to do. It usually only lasts for a few days, but I really hate feeling like I'm sneaking around behind his back. Most of the time, our relationship is different, very positive and completely supportive. When we have these minor disagreements, I try to hurry through what I think needs to be done, so I can get on with what he wants me to do. It is not a comfortable situation, and I would feel much better if we could agree on my work priorities all the time.

Katherine Huston has found that an organization's political culture is sometimes affected by its geographical location.

I found that Xerox in Rochester had many down-to-earth, midwestern values like honesty, integrity, and courtesy. In contrast, a large metropolitan company I worked for had a much more aggressive, confrontational style. The problem with this aggressive culture is that, when there are conflicts, it can be difficult to confront the issues in a positive way and get back on track. I saw a television program recently that showed that when a wolf is angry with another wolf for some reason, it will bite the nose of the offending wolf, and they will then work things out between them. The whole process is quick and apparently effective. I have worked in at least two organizations where the culture favored avoiding conflict rather than dealing with it.

Danger!

Stay clear of any political activity or conflict in which the following occur.

● The battle has no strategic value or impact on your performance.

● The situation does not support or contribute to one of your company's objectives.

● Your opponent is losing or looking bad by not playing fairly.

Although communication is important at all times, it is most important when there are disagreements and problems. Without it, you and coworkers can get stuck in nonproductive or counterproductive activities that will keep you from accomplishing your goals. Time and energy can be wasted avoiding, denying, or minimizing significant issues that should be resolved. The most successful work groups depend on strong interpersonal communication skills to build cooperation and collaboration.

Here are some general suggestions that can help you.

● Listening is an extremely important communication skill. To be effective, you need to be mentally and physically prepared to listen. You need to be willing to encourage the other person to express his or her point of view. That means you often need to withhold giving your opinion until you are sure you have heard and understood the other person.

- When someone is sending you a message, you need to remember that the message usually contains two elements: *content* and *feeling*. To make sure you really understand the complete message, try to repeat or rephrase, in your own words, what the other person is feeling and trying to say. It is a good way to avoid jumping to conclusions or getting into an argument. You can respond without either rejecting or accepting what has been said. Your initial intention is to make sure you understand the message. Paraphrasing or restating gives the other person a chance to clarify the message if you have misunderstood it.

- Sometimes you need to ask open, direct questions to make sure you understand what another person is saying and feeling. Use questions like: How do you feel about . . . ? What do you think of . . . ? In your opinion, how should we . . . ?

Since these questions cannot be answered with a simple yes or no response, they let other people know you want to hear more about their opinions and feelings—even if they don't agree with yours. Accepting the person's right to have a point of view does not mean you automatically agree. As a listener, you can very easily sabotage other people's ability to share their feelings and information with you if you do not demonstrate your willingness to at least accept what they have to say.

When there are problems or conflicts, use a problem-centered approach which gives the other person a sense of control over the problem and provides an open climate for communication. Instead of making the other person feel dominated or manipulated, try to concentrate on encouraging the individual to participate in solving the problem. Assigning blame or making subjective comments about a person usually causes defensive behavior and hampers a problem-solving approach. Using nonevaluative comments, which simply state that a problem exists, usually allows both parties to jointly discuss possible solutions.

Shortcut

To create a problem-solving atmosphere that encourages the sharing of information, try establishing ground rules to discuss the conflict. For example, you may want to set guidelines like those given in the following list.

- Everyone will be open and honest.

- Everyone will have a say and be heard.

- Everyone will listen to each other without argument or negative reaction and will keep a positive attitude.

- Opinions and feelings must be supported by facts or examples of specific behaviors or actions.

Remember these action steps for resolving a conflict.

1. Summarize your understanding of the situation.
   - How important is the issue and your need to resolve it?
   - What is your relationship with the other person?
   - What impact is this conflict having on that relationship?
   - What is the value to you or others to resolve this conflict?

2. Determine the best way to approach the other person.
   - How much time are you willing or able to spend on this issue?
   - What is the best way for you to deal with the conflict at this time?
   - How will the other person deal with this situation?

3. Meet with the other person.
   - Define the problem objectively and focus on quality, time, and cost factors.
   - Clarify your position by stating what you need (your non-negotiables).

- Acknowledge the other person's position and be sure that you really disagree with his or her point of view.
- Consider the bigger picture by discussing future implications or the impact on others if the conflict is not resolved effectively.
- List and evaluate as many options as possible to resolve the conflict.
- Select the best option and make sure that you are both willing to try this solution.
- Agree on the best way to monitor, evaluate, and reinforce a positive solution.

4. Implement your approach and review the outcomes.

- What did you gain or lose for now?
- What will you gain or lose in the future?
- What did the other person gain or lose?
- What will the other person gain or lose in the future?
- How do you both feel about this outcome?
- What would you do differently the next time?

Be assertive when you need to be. Deal with interpersonal conflicts quickly and effectively. Do not avoid confronting people and issues that are having a negative impact on *your* performance. How well you influence others depends on your credibility, how trustworthy you appear to others, and how much they respect you. It is possible for you to dramatically diminish the respect others have for you if you do not deal with conflict in a timely and effective way. Allowing a problem or issue to simmer or grow between you and someone else can have a negative impact on the two of you and everyone else who interacts with you. Conflicts can distract you and cause an uncomfortable working environment for others. You may need to take initiatives to handle potential or actual problems and maintain constructive relationships at all levels of your organization.

Some people may beat you and play games with your work relationship. Game playing includes many types of manipulative behavior that can disrupt operations, damage teamwork, distract supervisors, and destroy morale. In most cases, confrontation is required. You need to tell the person how disruptive the behavior is and that it must be changed. You need to try to channel unacceptable behavior toward a more acceptable approach. For example, you may have to insist to someone who is spreading rumors about you that he or she come talk to you first if they have questions or concerns. If the game playing continues, you may need to suggest that you will have to get outside help (from someone like your supervisor) to resolve the issue productively.

Don't Forget

When you are dealing with a difficult person, follow these guidelines.

- Remain calm. Do not argue or accuse.

- Listen carefully and make sure you clearly understand what the other person is saying.

- Be firm about your position. Decide in advance what behavior you will and will not accept.

- Be persistent and consistent in your approach so that the difficult person knows you are serious about the problem.

- Look for ways to lessen your exposure to the problem behavior or to reduce the causes of the behavior.

- Identify other people who can be supportive, objective, and helpful to you when this difficult person's behavior has disrupted or upset you.

Assertiveness increases your ability to influence others. People rarely need to wonder if you are being honest with them. When people know they are dealing with the real you, they tend to listen more attentively. When people listen more carefully to what you have to say, you are able to influence them more effectively. They don't have to spend valuable time and energy wondering about your reaction to a specific situation. They know that you will level with them and get down to business.

Assertiveness encourages people to want to work with you. They know that they will not have to worry about personal attacks, finger-pointing, or scapegoating. They know that you have a reputation for sticking to business, solving problems, and resolving interpersonal conflicts that stand in the way of getting work done. Assertiveness makes it easier for people to believe and trust you. Being assertive does not necessarily mean others will like you. But they will respect you.

An assertive approach lets you:

- Confront issues, problems, and behaviors—not people or personalities.

- State and discuss your feelings which leads to relieved tension, clearing the air, and prevention of a slow burn or a sudden blowup.

- Keep control. You can guide the way you want the relationship to continue, what you want to do and why. Stating your objectives and wishes brings clarity to your future work relationship with this person because the other person knows where you stand, and there is room for discussion.

Consistent and honest assertive communication establishes you as a credible, trustworthy person. You will be perceived as straightforward and clear about how you perceive things, how you discuss them, and how you are willing to make things work.

If you need to take assertive action, follow these suggestions.

- Pick a time and place when you feel you are in control.

- Prepare yourself by deciding what you want to say and how you want to say it. Consider rehearsing with a friend. Practice your opening words and make mental notes about the key points you want to make.

- Be direct. Get to the point quickly and stay focused on your main ideas.
- Use *I* statements to describe your feelings and priorities.
- Don't ask for feedback unless (or until) you are ready to turn the conversation over to the other person.
- Speak firmly and confidently. Make sure that your body language (posture, eye contact, gestures, facial expressions) matches your message. Your nonverbal communication should be consistent with your verbal messages.
- Ask for the other person's reaction. Instead of guessing, wondering, or assuming how the other person feels, asking a simple question like "So what do you think about what I've said?" can show that you value the other's feeling and can open the door for a two-way dialogue.

Remember these action steps for confronting an interpersonal problem.

1. Set up a private meeting and allow sufficient time to discuss the problem.
2. Describe the inappropriate behavior in a nonaccusatory way and emphasize why it concerns you.
   - Use specific facts and examples.
   - Don't offer your opinion about the possible cause of the problem.
   - Focus on the behavior, not on the person or on personalities.
3. Listen carefully to check your understanding of the problem and its causes.
4. Ask clarifying questions to confirm your understanding.
5. Ask probing questions (especially with quiet, thoughtful, or shy people) and encourage them to respond by being patient and silent.

6. State the change in behavior that you want from the other person. Be clear about what you need and be willing to compromise if another alternative seems workable.

7. Agree on a specific action plan.

8. Set a follow-up date to review and recognize progress.

Assertiveness is the ability to express your feelings to define how you will act in particular situations, to speak up for opinions you believe in, to show self-confidence, to disagree when you think it is important to do so, to ask others to change their behavior, and to carry out plans for modifying your own behavior.

Assertive behavior can help you get what you want more often. But you also need to cooperate with others to help them get what they want, too. You need to balance assertive behavior with responsive or cooperative behavior. Every relationship, every interaction has two sides, two sets of needs and interests, two people asserting or describing what is important to them. Without listening and responding effectively to each other, there would be conflict, disagreement, and a stressful working relationship. By balancing assertive behavior with responsive behavior, you will:

- Ask how the other person sees the situation.

- Ask about the other person's feelings and try to understand them (even if you don't agree).

- Identify ways you may need to change your behavior to improve the situation or relationship especially if you learn that something you are doing is inappropriate, ineffective, or counterproductive.

- Listen carefully to ideas from others that may help you do a better job and get the results you want.

In conflict situations, when you negotiate by instinct or intuition or use win-lose power plays, you risk reaching an agreement that is shortsighted, one-sided, or manipulative. You may win the argument and destroy the relationship. Here are some guidelines for balancing assertive and responsive behaviors to negotiate a fair agreement.

- Recognize the other person's position.
- Agree on the desired outcome.
- Collect data so that you know the facts.
- Set limits. Establish ground rules.
- Respect the other person's viewpoint.
- Find areas of mutual agreement or interest.
- Start on a positive note.
- Prepare for the meeting and carry through with your plan.
- Foster a give-and-take, question-and-answer exchange.
- Stay focused on your objective.
- Develop alternatives and compromises.
- Summarize key points.
- End on a positive note.

Most conflicts can be resolved effectively if you are willing to approach the other person in a spirit of cooperation and collaboration. The following techniques can often bring mutually satisfactory results:

- Describe the problem as you see it. Explain what is happening in your own words. Use specific, recent examples to clarify your interpretation of the situation.
- Explain the impact the problem is having on your performance. Let the other person know that the situation is serious enough for the two of you to address and resolve it. Use specific examples: "I'm missing important deadlines," "We are running over budget," or "Our production level is down."
- Ask for and listen to the other person's perspective. Get the whole picture before you try to resolve the problem. Be willing to understand what the other person needs or wants to make the sit-

uation better. Encourage participation and reach agreement about the nature, scope, and urgency of the problem. Building consensus about what is happening is the best way to begin identifying an appropriate long-lasting solution.

- Agree on the problem and its root causes. Analyzing what has happened and why it has happened can provide a solid understanding about what has to happen next. Workable solutions often emerge from collaborative conversations based on mutual trust and respect. Some greater good often emerges as the basis for a win-win solution that neither person may have thought of at the beginning of the discussion.

- Identify and prioritize possible solutions. List as many options as you can. Be open-minded and nonjudgmental as possible. This informal brainstorming is a good starting point to explore a range of opportunities and alternatives. After you have exhausted your list of ideas, work with the other person to combine, eliminate, or refine possible solutions. This collaborative activity will often lead to a few workable solutions from which a best one can be selected.

- Implement and monitor the solution. Agree on an action plan that includes ways for you to measure progress and recognize success. The only way to know if the problem has been completely resolved is to follow up with each other periodically. Decide now what is the best way to keep in touch with each other (when, where, how) about whether the conflict has been resolved to your mutual satisfaction.

In *The 1988 Annual: Developing Human Resources,* Beverly Byrum defines assertiveness as "a communication technique designed to demonstrate respect toward self and others and to allow the expression of a full range of behaviors." Assertiveness does not mean anything goes; it is not synonymous with being aggressive, pushy, or domineering. Assertiveness is generally defined as "the ability to express oneself honestly without denying the rights of others." Our rights also have corresponding responsibilities: our right to be listened to requires that we listen to others and honor their right to be heard; our right to be respected for our thoughts and feelings requires that we respect the ideas of others; our right to be assertive without feeling guilty requires that we encourage others to be open with us and accept the feedback we receive from them.

Conflict is an inevitable by-product of human interactions. If we are willing to be both assertive and cooperative in our dealings with others, we can reach collaborative solutions that have long-lasting benefits to everyone involved.

It's a Wrap

✔ Conflict does not have to be negative or disabling. If you are open to new ideas and willing to collaborate with others, conflict can broaden your perspective and present possibilities you may never have thought about before.

✔ Communication skills (especially your ability and willingness to listen) are essential when dealing with conflict or when confronting a difficult person whose behavior is problematic to you. Understanding the nature, scope, and cause of the problem is critical to finding a suitable solution.

✔ If you cannot successfully resolve a conflict you are having with someone else, you may need to enlist the help of a third party who can provide an objective, rational, and nonemotional alternative to the problem. Sometimes you are too close to the situation to see a viable option that will have broader, longer-lasting value to you, the other person, and your organization.

CHAPTER 9

POLITICAL TECHNIQUE 7

Take Charge of Your Own Morale and Your Own Career

It is not the mountain we conquer, but ourselves.—**Sir Edmund Hilary**

The good life is a process, not a state of being. It is a direction, not a destination.—**Carl Rogers**

Do I Need to Read This Chapter?

➡ Do you have a clear idea about the work you want to do or the position you want to have three years from now?

➡ Do you know what it will take for you to get where you want to be in the next three to five years?

➡ What are you currently doing to empower or enable yourself to manage your own performance and your own career?

In *The Change Masters,* Rosabeth Moss Kanter states that three basic *power tools* must be available if companies want their employees to "reach outside of and beyond the authority of position to develop ideas for change." These power tools are:

- *Information* (data, technical knowledge, political savvy, expertise)
- *Resources* (funds, materials, space, time)
- *Support* (endorsement, backing, approval, recognition)

These are the tools you need to get from your supervisors and managers so that you can empower yourself when appropriate opportunities arise.

You must maintain a high degree of self-esteem, accept responsibility for the job you are being paid to do, feel part of a team, and believe you are involved in something important, relevant, or useful. In *The Empowered Manager,* Peter Block describes empowerment as "an act of faith. We commit ourselves to operate in a way that we believe in because it is what we have to do. Other people's experience may act as signposts for us, but we take the trip alone."

The more you take responsibility for your own actions, your own morale, and your own career, the more you will be able to apply your talents and resources to tasks that will help you be more successful. You are in control of your actions and reactions, and you have both the opportunity and the responsibility to manage your own destiny. Others will have an impact on your efforts, but you are ultimately the person in control. Self-discipline means regulating your behavior for the sake of self-improvement and future achievement. It means keeping the proper perspective about what is going on today so that you are alert and ready for tomorrow's challenges and opportunities.

The good news is that your work does not have to be a daily grind or a painful experience. As John Gardner reminds us in *Morale:*

The truth is that most human beings are so constructed that they want something active to do, something that tests them, that engages

---

Don't Forget

- Keep a positive attitude and outlook. Approach your job with enthusiasm and dedication. Change what you can about your work to keep it interesting and challenging. Change what you can about yourself to make sure you are giving your employer a full day's work.

---

their mind and their will, that involves not only effort but purposefulness. If they are paid for it, it's called work, and they're not supposed to enjoy it—but many do. It's a shocking thought, but there it is.

In talking with new employees, Carol Tunstall, a human resource manager, suggests a similar frame of reference.

Do something you enjoy and get satisfaction from your work. Don't depend too much on external rewards. Know yourself well enough to go after opportunities you really want. Stay open to new situations and look for opportunities to grow and expand, even if you have to make some sacrifices in the short term.

Get exposure to people outside your area. Many jobs are filled internally through referrals or with known people. For example, at one point in my career, I was working as a statistician consulting with a management team. I learned that they would be filling a quality manager position. I had some ideas about how to set up that position, and I met with one of the team members to express those ideas. I saw a way to make a contribution and have an impact on the business. They offered me the job, and I took it.

Also, look to the future and make yourself marketable outside your own organization. You are responsible for your own career. You can't depend on the company to take care of you. Today, younger people expect to make several career changes. My caution is not to let visions of the future interfere with your ability to establish your reputation and credibility by delivering on promises and commitments and finding ways to do your job better.

Quick Tips

Use the career worksheet illustrated in Fig. 9.1 to analyze obstacles and gaps in your career plan. Start at the bottom with your current job, and work your way toward the top, the future position you want. The following questions may help you determine where you are, where you want to be, and what you need to do to prepare for your next opportunity.

- What are you doing now and how is your current job helping you prepare for the future?

- What do you want to be doing three to five years from now?

- Is there a specific job in your company that will provide you the opportunity to do what you want to be doing? Are you already in that job? If the job does not exist, will you have to lobby to have it created or will you have to look for your ideal opportunity somewhere else?

- If the job you want is different from the job you have, what competencies or skills will you need for the future? Do you currently have any of these competencies? How will you develop the necessary skills required to qualify for your ideal future job?

- Are there many people in line for or interested in the job you want? How serious is the competition, and how good are your competing coworkers? What do you need to do to make sure the right decision makers know you are interested in the position? What do you need to do to ensure them that you are qualified (or getting qualified) for that position?

- What are the realistic odds that you will get the position you want in your current company? Is it worth it to you to develop the skills you need for your next position? Do you have a practical development plan that your current supervisor will support? Can you get ready for your future job and still do exceptional work in your current job?

Success is not an accident. It means being in the right place at the right time ready to do the right thing. Stay current about what's

CAREER WORKSHEET: IDENTIFYING GAPS

FUTURE POSITION

- Duties & Responsibilities
- Competencies & Skills Required
- Availability

POSSIBLE ISSUES OR CONCERNS

- Support from Key Decision Makers
- Extent of Competition from Coworkers or External Resources
- Development Plan to Ensure Readiness for Next Position

CURRENT POSITION

- Duties & Responsibilities
- Competencies & Skills Required
- Opportunity to Develop Skills for Next Position

Figure 9.1

going on in your company, industry, and profession. There are several things you can do.

- Talk to people in your company. Go to meetings with an open mind and listen to what others have to say.

- Talk to people in your profession. Attend association meetings or special events that bring you into contact with others who are doing what you do for a living.

- Talk to people in your industry. Pay attention to what they have to say about trends or isolated incidents that are affecting their business.

- Get comfortable and competent with the latest information technology.

Political savvy in pursuit of a promotion or a climb up the corporate ladder requires some preparation on your part. Determine from the start that fair play will be nonnegotiable. Seek out those people who would benefit by your good performance and enlist their help in your preparation. Conversely, avoid those people whose performance track record has been poor or who stand to lose ground by your advancement.

Once you have determined the job you want to aim for, it is important to make a complete and brutally honest self-assessment.

- Why do you want that job? Is it something you would do well? Why?
- What skills does that job require that you don't presently have? How can you get them?
- On what could you base your request for the new job? What would the company gain from your being in that position?

Once you have made your honest self-assessment, ask those whose opinions and counsel you trust (coworkers, managers, and associates) to further evaluate your skills and give you *their* honest feedback. List both those assets and shortcomings you have discovered about yourself.

Plan a course of action you need to take to fill in the skills you are lacking for that job.

1. Do you need further technical skills? What do you need to do to get them? Is there training offered in your own organization that would help you get these skills? If not, would you need to attend classes on your own time and at your own expense to get these skills? Are you willing to do this?

2. Do you need to be comfortable with other interpersonal skills (communication, writing, public speaking)? Again, are there courses offered within your own company that would help you with these? If not, would you need to attend classes on your own time and at your own expense to get these skills? Are you willing to do this?

3. Is your present professional appearance and demeanor aligned with the image the company wants to project?

An assistant branch manager at our local bank recently got several tattoos on her hands. Although she is the same confident and capable worker she has been for years, we have noticed a few customers going to other personnel rather than to her for their banking needs. She no longer personifies the professional they once could trust with their money. Same person, different image.

If you don't think that image and dress are important, imagine entrusting yourself to a surgeon with a pierced nose and fatigues or to an airline pilot who walks into the cockpit wearing a bathing suit. Sounds funny, but you would judge their capability by the image they project.

Maybe there are people within your organization whose professional appearance and behavior seem to typify the company's definition of confidence and capability. They may be flattered if you enlist their opinions about what you might need to do to improve your own style. If not, there are many courses offered at local evening classes on creating a professional image.

4. If you are aspiring to a job with more customer contact, are your social skills polished and professional? Try to remember a time in your own life when you were the customer and got poor service. If given the option, would you ever return to that store or would you take your business elsewhere?

Can you exercise patience with difficult people? Do you get satisfaction from working through a problem in order to give a customer better service?

And in your speech, do you avoid the use of slang? Do you regularly use ethnic, racial, sexist, or other derogatory terms in speaking with others? Would you be proud of your interactions with others if they were played back to you on videotape?

5. How could you sell yourself to get that position you want? If you were to get the new job, what assets do you possess that would make you especially valuable to the organization? Are you able to offer the company something more than the basic job description demands? In other words, why should *you* above anyone else get this job? If you can answer honestly that the skills you have mastered would make you the best person for the job, go for it! If not, what more can you do to make yourself the perfect choice?

Get Started

To gain and maintain control of your professional success:

- Stay focused on business issues.

- Be innovative and flexible.

- Involve others early and often.

- Test your ideas using standard criteria: quantity, quality, cost, and time.

- Don't ignore, deny, or minimize problems.

- Don't avoid conflict with people who have a major impact on your job performance.

- Don't hesitate to act when your intuition tells you that benefits outweigh costs.

- Don't dwell on mistakes. Learn from them and get back on track as quickly as you can.

- Accept the fact that damage control may be the best you can do sometimes.

Susan McKeone, an internal consultant, feels that doing good work gets you noticed.

I encourage people to distinguish between what's in the foreground and what's in the background. For me, the foreground is my work—

what I can do for the company. The background is what the company should do for me because of the value of that work. Doing the best work I can is my primary responsibility and my number one priority. People need to take charge of their own career but not in a way that is too mechanistic. Their careers should be in the background of their work. It's a balancing act. You need to network not just for your career but for your work. People I work with speak well about me because I do my work well, and they know I want to do good work for them—the benefits to my career are an end result.

Fred Gauss, contract audit supervisor for the city of Philadelphia, decided early in his career that the best way to get ahead was to prove that he could produce.

I knew I had to make a positive impression by doing quality work. If I did that, I could go with the flow and everything would work out. Because I did good work, I got exposure to the top people in our office. Because I worked hard for my boss, he took care of me in return. The one piece of advice I would pass on to others is never to use "that's not my job" as an excuse for not doing a little extra. Even if you work in a very regimented office, you need to help people get the information they need, even if it's outside your usual job description.

There are several things you can do to increase your professional value.

1. Do your current job to the best of your ability. Identify your strengths and make the best use of your strongest talents. Be a consistent, reliable performer. Hold yourself accountable for your own job performance. Set high personal standards and meet or beat them.

2. Be a professional in your behavior, attitude, and approach to others. Be punctual, courteous, and committed to your organization's objectives. Share your successes and do not blame others for problems that you could have helped avoid or resolve. When you do a good job, be proud of your accomplishment, whether or not it is acknowledged by others. When you know you can do better, do better.

3. Show discipline and self-control. Do not let your emotions interfere with your work. Take a logical, thoughtful approach when problems occur. Confront difficult situations or people calmly, rationally, and constructively.

4. Project self-confidence and competence. Maintain an image of success in the way you look and in the way you organize your work area. Neatness in appearance sends a strong message to others that you take pride in yourself and your surroundings. The way you dress should be appropriate to your company's culture and your place in it. If there are special occasions (like a meeting with an executive) that require you to dress up a notch, you should know when and how to do so. If there are times (like casual Fridays) that permit you to dress down, you should know when and how far to go.

5. Be prepared to build and use a network of contacts. Keep business cards available and give them out to anyone you consider a useful, interesting, or potentially helpful contact. Let people know what you do. Selling yourself is often a simple matter of telling people about your work and why you enjoy doing what you do. Keep your initial networking conversations brief and courteous. Be sensitive to the other person's time and interests. First encounters are rarely the best time to get into lengthy discussions about your career interests. The best networkers plant many seeds before they worry about cultivating any of them. Time then tells them which relationships might be fruitful.

6. Expand your contact base by joining professional or social organizations. Golfing still ranks as one of the best networking activities in today's business world. But other strong connections have been made and strengthened through church groups, alumni associations, community activities like the Jaycees, or civic volunteer work like the United Way. Giving time to help a local nonprofit organization, offering your assistance to a neighborhood fundraising effort, or volunteering your time to teach or tutor at a nearby school can expand your network and improve your own base of experience. Some of these pursuits can enhance your pres-

ent résumé which you should always keep current and ready to hand out to the right people.

7. Find an advocate, sponsor, or mentor in your organization who is willing to help you with your career. Although one person may be able to do many things to help you, it often makes more sense to find a few people who are willing to be part of your support group. Your immediate supervisor should play an active role coaching and developing you. But you may also want to build connections with others who can champion your good ideas, speak out for you when opportunities arise, and offer you sound advice about what you need to do to succeed or advance in your company. Think of your boss as the primary source of support, and do not let your association with other supporters damage your relationship with your immediate supervisor. But cultivate your network of contacts in such a way that several people are on your side and willing to go to bat for you when the time comes.

8. Take calculated risks with your career. Accept new challenges that you are ready (or at least nearly ready) to tackle. Know which assignments or opportunities have the greatest potential for failure, and develop a strategy to avoid them or to minimize the probable negative outcomes. Contingency planning involves understanding what can possibly go wrong with a particular task and then deciding what you can do to prevent a problem from occurring or to control the damage if the problem cannot be avoided. Sometimes a little planning can produce proactive alternatives that will make an apparently risky assignment safer and more manageable.

9. Keep track of your own accomplishments and successes. Start and maintain a file that documents your contributions to your company's goals. Use objective language to describe what you have done: "Finished the ABC project three weeks ahead of schedule," "Implemented a quality control process that will save our department $7500 per year," "Resolved a customer's complaint successfully and saved their $100,000 annual contract with our company." This information may be important when you are applying for a

promotion within your company or developing a résumé for a new job somewhere else.

10. Know your competition and be honest about your chances to get ahead. With today's downsizing and reengineering activities, there are fewer advancement opportunities and more individuals aspiring to them. Going upward on your company's organization chart may not be the best course for you to pursue. Going in another direction may make more sense now than ever before. A lateral move, for example, might expand your skills, give you a broader base of experience for future opportunities, and provide you with more interesting challenges than you might have gotten with a promotion. We also know individuals who have taken a step or two backward to sharpen their sales or computer skills in order to improve their chances for longer-term advancement. Know what is important to you and factor in these motivators whenever you evaluate your current level of job satisfaction. Be realistic about what you can do and what you need to do better in order to stay career-competitive with your peers.

Remember that you are seeking job satisfaction and pursuing career advancement in a specific work environment with an established culture. Unless you are self-employed, you are working with others and perhaps even competing with them for available opportunities.

And the competition is heating up in many organizations. As Rosabeth Kanter points out in *When Giants Learn to Dance:*

> For much of the recent past, the idea of a career in the business world meant to most people a series of almost-automatic promotions to bigger and better jobs inside a company. Such a bureaucratic career pattern is defined by the logic of *advancement*. The bureaucratic career path involves a sequence of positions in a defined hierarchy of positions. At the same time that traditional career ladders are being built at the bottom the higher rungs are being lopped off. More people at lower levels have *theoretical* access to promotion while the

actual number of slots "above" is declining. The survivors of restructuring efforts are thus well aware that while they may still have a *job,* they may no longer have a *career*—at least in the traditional sense.

Communication Manager Steve Ozer remembers when companies used to have career centers.

People would help you decide on a career path and recommend the right steps to take. Today, you can't wait for someone to guide you. Deliver what you are being paid to do, but volunteer to do something outside your current job. Pick something that is strategically important to you. Managing your own career means knowing what you're good at and what you're not good at, and filling the gaps. You need to assess your own skills in a very direct and honest way. When I did that, 11 years ago, I realized I was terrified of public speaking. Had I not done anything about it, I would have plateaued around 10 years ago. I decided that I needed to do something about that—I kept trying to get out of things rather than confronting them. Finally, I worked on the problem diligently for two years—and I've had three or four promotions during that time.

To have a position of greater influence, public speaking—convincing others of the value of a project in a group setting or meeting—was a critical competency. That was an honest assessment of a weakness that required action. You have to keep doing that, you have to keep asking yourself, "What else? What next?" And sometimes you need third party help with your skill assessments. Obviously your manager should be doing some of that, but peers can also help you out with honest, timely feedback.

Don't Forget

- Let others know how you feel and what you are thinking, but be optimistic about what you have to say. In the words of a favorite grandfather, "Brighten the corner where you are." Look for and talk about the positives. If you don't have anything good to say—listen!

Whenever you evaluate your current level of job satisfaction and gauge how ready you are for new opportunities, there are a variety of factors you may want to consider.

- The amount of power, control, authority, and influence you have.
- How much respect, recognition, or praise you receive.
- How much status you get from your work demonstrated by money, promotion, or job title.
- How much teamwork, trust, and friendship you get in your job.
- The number of new projects and challenging work assignments available to you.

Set professional goals for yourself at least twice a year and evaluate your progress every six months. When you review your achievements, you may decide to:

- Maintain your current level of performance in your current job.
- Improve your current level of performance in order to keep your current job or to qualify for a new one.
- Change your job, the company you work for, or your overall work objective.

Research suggests that most people go through four major career stages during their lives. Figure 9.2 illustrates these traditional progressions which for many people follow a fairly predictable chronological order. However, more and more people are pursuing entrepreneurial opportunities and finding job satisfaction in lateral moves or completely different work activities. For example, we know an individual who started out as a high school teacher, went to work for 10 years in a large commercial bank, left that job to help an associate start and build a successful company, and is currently, at age 54, writing history books. He describes his career progression as "a cycle of activity that has brought him to the job he has always wanted." Another person we know retired from her nursing career at age 49 to try her hand at computer technology. Almost 15 years later, she is self-employed and maintains an active, rewarding schedule with a select group of satisfied clients.

The important thing to remember today is that there are a greater number of work options available in our global economy. There are many smaller companies now which provide opportunities that were once available only in large corporations. Successful entrepreneurial ventures are more common that ever before, and people are finding creative ways to make their work a more meaningful part of their lives.

When you review your current level of job satisfaction, make sure that it is consistent with your overall sense of purpose. Are the demands and challenges of your work providing adequate financial

TRADITIONAL CAREER STAGES

STAGE ONE	STAGE TWO	STAGE THREE	STAGE FOUR
Orientation & Investigation	Planning for Advancement	Talented Resource	Trusted Expert
Trying various job activities, assessing your level of satisfaction, beginning to identify options beyond your initial position.	Identifying what challenges you, developing competence in a specialty area, dealing with failures, finding support, defining "what's next?"	Developing a broader view of work and your role in your organization or profession.	Passing on your knowledge and skills, becoming a leader, mentor, or adviser in your company or field.
Age 18–25	Age 25–35	Age 35–50	Age 50– Retirement

Figure 9.2

and psychological rewards? Are you still having fun doing what you are being paid to do? Do you look forward to going to work each day because you enjoy your job and the people you work with? Figure 9.3 lists some factors that can help you evaluate your current level of job satisfaction. If things seem out of balance, revise your plans to shift direction, accelerate your progress, or negotiate for a different alternative. Be optimistic and upbeat. Bertrand Russell has described what most of us are looking for.

> If you look about you at the men and women whom you can call happy, you will see that they all have certain things in common. The most important of these things is an activity which at most times is enjoyable on its own account, and which, in addition, gradually builds up into something that you are glad to see coming into existence.

Shortcut

- Always have a clear idea about the jobs and career paths that are available to you within your company, your industry, your profession. Keep an updated list of possible employers (including the company you currently work for) and contacts at two or three of your company's main competitors.

Steve Foster, Rohm and Haas human resource manager, encourages employees to pursue a variety of interests.

> I had a great mentor when I first started out. When you work with someone who sets a good example, the experience stays with you forever. What I learned and would recommend to others is to adopt a generalist approach to your career early on, then narrow your focus later by selecting a few jobs or specialties you want to be known for. People who can only toss one ball in the air or into a basket are often the ones who become targets during downsizing or restructuring activities. Today, people need transferable skills to move across organizational lines.

SELF-ASSESSMENT: YOUR CURRENT LEVEL OF JOB SATISFACTION

	HIGH	MEDIUM	LOW
1. The amount of power, control, authority, and influence you have.			
2. How much respect, recognition or praise you receive.			
3. How much status you get from your work demonstrated by money, promotion, or job title.			
4. How much teamwork, trust, and friendship you get in your job.			
5. The number of new projects and challenging work assignments available to you.			

Your conclusions:

Figure 9.3

Aleene Maiaroto, mortgage loan officer for a large commercial bank, describes the importance of taking charge of your own career development.

Because I came up through small companies, I came from a background where I thought of what I did as a job, not a career. When I got to a big company, I had a mentor who took me from being a processor to being a corporate trainer. He believed in me and recommended me for a job. I rode on his coattails for a while until I got confidence in my own skills. But when the company got bigger and bigger, I couldn't wait around to be recognized. I realized I had to figuratively stand on my desk and shout, "I'm a good person, and you're lucky to have me!" I had to be assertive and let people know: "This is what I'm up to." I put it in writing and passed it on to someone else. I learned to align myself with others and make myself known. At office parties and social functions, I would say hello to the company president and other executives. I also volunteered for things, mostly those touchy-feely things that I knew I would be good at doing.

Sometimes, people above me don't make smart or fair decisions. That can be demoralizing. For example, we have a terrific salesperson in our office, and the company idolizes him. As a result, he gets certain privileges that are inequitable. I finally had to say to myself, "that's him, and I can't worry about it." I have to make sure my needs are getting met and then not worry about others. I need to do a good job for me.

My advice for young people today: be flexible. Learn as much as you can. If you know several things, you add value in different ways and get to stay at the office when others are being asked to stay home. Be as diverse as possible—answer phones, sell products or services, process loans—pick two or three things you like to do and go learn how to do them well.

Although there may be others who are competing with you for key projects or positions, your relationship with them does not have to be hostile or mean-spirited. As Steven Covey points out in *Principle-Centered Leadership:*

By acting on the assumption others want and mean to do their best, as they see it, you can exert a powerful influence and bring out the best in them. Each person has many dimensions and potentials, some in evidence, most dormant. And they tend to respond to how we treat them and what we believe about them. Whenever we assume good faith, born of good motives and inner security, we appeal to the good in others.

Danger!

- Avoid falling into the trap of depending on others to manage your work, your development, and your career. In some cases, they are too busy. In other cases, what they want for themselves or for you may not be what you want. Ask for help, but stay in charge of your own work life.

On a more practical level, Marianne Gauss recalls some specific steps she needed to take to rise above the fray and manage her own morale.

I started out as a bank auditor in 1975. It was the beginning of a lot of gender-sensitivity issues in the country and in the business world. There were only four women in our department; there were no women in the hierarchy above us. One of the women kept a book about every gender incident in the department. When these things happened to me, I would tell people right to their face to stop, and it wouldn't be a problem for me anymore. One morning she started talking about how she had been slighted or offended by a new job assignment, and I finally said, "I can't do this anymore—I can't buy into this downward spiral of negativity. If you have a legitimate complaint, I'll work with you to try to get it resolved, but I think you are overreacting with some of these problems, assuming malice, and taking things personally when they're not meant to be." From then on, I was able to keep a positive perspective on my work, and I realized I'm responsible for my own morale.

I have been involved with various types of hazing from some of my male counterparts, but I try not to automatically assume that certain behaviors are discrimination or gender bias. If you think it is, you need to confront it. For me to be competent and professional, I need to be upbeat and confident about what's going on around me. If things aren't going well, I think about the worst-case scenario, and then I develop a strategy to deal with that extreme. Usually I can keep things in perspective. I choose to remember the *boost* things and forget the bad times.

Johanna Zitto encourages people to go over and above the call of duty.

Try to top your own personal best. You place the bar where it is challenging for you and then top it. Pick your spots and go for it. When you wonder "why should I bother?" the answer should be "because that's the way you are." That's what will differentiate you from others.

Henry David Thoreau once offered this wise counsel:

If a man advances confidently in the direction of his dreams to live the life he has imagined, he will meet with a success unexpected in common hours.

It's a Wrap

✔ Success is not an accident. You have control over your current job, your future work, and the level of satisfaction you get from what you do to earn a living. Keep your job in perspective—it is not your life, only an important part of it.

✔ Set professional goals for yourself at least twice a year. Review your progress every six months and, if you are not satisfied with where you are, determine what you need to do to make a change. Continue doing acceptable work in your current job while you launch your campaign to find or create a better job for yourself.

✔ Stay optimistic about your current situation and your future prospects. There is a self-fulfilling prophesy aspect to your career. If you honestly believe you can have a satisfying work life, you will be open to new opportunities and sought out by people in authority who see you as enthusiastic and approachable.

POLITICAL TECHNIQUE 8
Maintain a Sense of Humor

The joy of joys is the person of light but unmalicious humor.
—**Emily Post,** *Etiquette: The Blue Book of Social Usage*

Humor helps us through the hard times and makes the good times better. It enhances communication, enables learning, defuses anger, promotes productivity and mediates stress. A light-hearted approach to life will give you a more optimistic outlook and a cheerful way of relating to others.
—**Lila Green,** *Making Sense of Humor*

Do I Need to Read This Chapter?

➡ Are you able to keep your work in perspective, or are there more and more occasions when living and what you do *for* a living have become synonymous?

➡ How skillfully are you dealing with occasional or routine work pressures? Do you often find yourself taking work worries home with you?

➡ Are you able to be affable, friendly, and cordial at work even when you are faced with problems, conflicts, and crises?

In a recent *Philadelphia Inquirer* article (15 December 1997), Lila Green reports that:

> According to a book of averages, the average pre-school child laughs 250 times a day. The average adult, only 15 times a day. We lose a lot of laughter between childhood and adulthood. As we grow up and take on more responsibilities, we start taking ourselves very seriously. But if you've let your sense of humor fall by the wayside, you've let a vital and healthy part of yourself atrophy. You're missing out, not just on good times and laughter, but on one of the most efficient, effective, readily available, inexpensive, safest stress-relievers around. Take your work in life seriously, but take yourself lightly, because those who laugh . . . last!

Many of us are now familiar with the important research Norman Cousins documented in his battle with an incurable disease over 20 years ago. He discovered that a positive emotional outlook enhances both physical and psychological healing and that sustained laughter stimulates an increased release of endorphins—the body's natural morphine. In *An Anatomy of an Illness,* Mr. Cousin describes the benefits of a good laugh.

> Some people, in the grip of uncontrollable laughter, say their ribs are hurting. The expression is probably accurate, but it is a delightful "hurt" that leaves the individual relaxed almost to the point of an open sprawl. It is the kind of "pain," too, that most people would do well to experience every day of their lives. It is as specific and tangible as any other form of physical exercise. Though its biochemical manifestations have yet to be as explicitly charted and understood as the effects of fear or frustration or rage, they are real enough.

Laughter can truly be the best medicine for our daily aches, pains, and worries. Other research studies support the value of humor in our daily lives. Dr. William Fry's work at Stanford University provides convincing evidence that laughter strengthens the heart muscle and helps some people lower their blood pressure. Dr. Fry's work has shown that just 20 minutes of laughter is the cardiovascular equivalent of three minutes of strenuous rowing. Ashley Montagu has written more than 50 books and credits his long career to *neoteny*—childlike behaviors like curiosity, flexibility, spontaneity, playfulness, and creativity that can help adults live longer, healthier, more fulfilling lives. In fact, there are volumes of research supporting what Hippocrates realized thousands of years ago: there is a strong link between mind and body, between our spirit and our health, between improving a patient's outlook on life and healing the body.

We all make choices every day about how we will tackle that day's challenges. We have all worked with some coworkers who continually bring their same problems to and from work each day. They project a "woe is me" attitude. Murphy's Law ("Whatever can go wrong, will go wrong") seems to be the baggage they drag from place to place. Be warned! For your own sanity and for your own peace of mind, avoid these doom-and-gloom people if you can. And if you can't avoid them, at least let them know you will not be brought down by their negative attitude. We once had a coworker who for a while announced at the beginning of each workday, "Don't hold me responsible for anything today, I'm in a bad mood." After about two weeks of this, her supervisor took her aside at the end of a workday and confronted this issue: "Whatever it is that's putting you in that bad mood, either get rid of it, or leave it at home. You're affecting the morale of everyone around you."

We all have also seen coworkers whose positive spirit is almost contagious. They are the ones who cheerfully seem to accept the challenges each day brings with renewed energy. They accomplish much because they expect to accomplish much. They are not brought down by minor defeats. These people are the ones we all like to work with. They inspire others around them to give their best and to enjoy the success these efforts bring. We see these cheer spreaders on assembly lines doing what many of us would consider monotonous routine jobs. We can see them in the crowded cubicles in large companies helping another coworker tackle a problem. We see them in the top floors of corporations where a simple "Great job!" inspires you to do even more.

No one expects you to be a Pollyanna. People who never have problems are probably not doing anything at all. It's mastering the defeats that make us better at the next task. One person we know calls these defeats *tuition.* He says, "I paid the price (in either time, effort, or money), and I learned something—just like college."

In *Lighten Up,* C. W. Metcalf and Roma Felible describe humor as both a set of skills and an outlook on the world that "can help you thrive in change, remain creative under pressure, work more effectively, play more enthusiastically, and stay healthier in the process." The authors emphasize the importance of learning three survival skills.

1. *The first humor skill: the ability to see the absurdity in difficult situations.* One of our business associates was asked at the last minute to represent his department at an important planning meeting. He assumed, incorrectly, that all he needed to do was show up, take notes, and bring back information to his manager. When he arrived at the meeting, he discovered he was the third speaker on the company president's agenda. He soon also found out that the first speaker had prepared overhead transparencies to accompany his 40-minute presentation. Knowing that his turn was coming up soon, he watched as others in the audience politely applauded the first speaker. While the second speaker droned on about quotas and production goals, our unprepared associate realized how absurd the situation was and determined a course of action. When it was his turn, he stopped on his way to the podium and wrote four words on a nearby flipchart: WHO, WHAT, WHEN, and WHY. He then explained his preference for journalistic brevity and precision and delivered a 10-minute extemporaneous explanation of the three key projects currently going on in his department. He was rewarded for his directness by enthusiastic clapping by his colleagues and a complimentary smile from the company president.

Get Started

1. Whether it's *Doonesbury* or *Dilbert, The Far Side* or *Family Circus,* start each day with a laugh—or at least a smile. Make it a point to read the comic section of your daily newspaper before you turn to the business, sports, or news sections.

2. When you see a magazine cartoon that makes you laugh, clip it out and put it where you will see it again some time when you really need it. Looking at a funny picture before you go out on an important sales call or before you start a serious planning meeting can help you keep things in perspective.

3. Keep a file of favorite jokes or humorous sayings and use them to set the tone for your meetings and interactions with others. If you are not comfortable telling a joke to start a presentation, at least try to lighten things up with something amusing, creative, or entertaining. Quoting some well-known humorist like Will Rogers or Mark Twain can often be effective.

4. When you are feeling unusual pressure or stress, take a step back to retain your composure and your perspective. Try to look at the big picture by asking yourself questions like: "What's the worst possible thing that could happen here, and what would it mean to me?" or "In the overall scheme of things, just how important is this next 20-minute meeting? What will this matter in 10 years?" Sometimes it is possible to see that your worst fears are not really that significant.

5. Develop a reputation as someone who can go with the flow and not be swept away by a tide of bad news or work pressures. A doom-and-gloom approach brings you and others down quickly. Remember, too, that self-fulfilling prophesies do occur: when you are sure that things can only get worse, they probably will. So believe that things will only get better and see what happens.

2. *The second humor skill: the ability to take yourself lightly while taking your work seriously.* Years ago, I was on the way to an important sales meeting with three other coworkers. The four of us were tense and anxious about this crucial contact. One of our colleagues stopped suddenly and did a two-minute take-off of Curley, his favorite member of the Three Stooges. He made a few "yuck-yuck" noises, waved his right hand in front of his face, and patted his head several times to get our attention. We all laughed, took a deep breath, and walked in to meet this important prospect with smiles on our faces and an air of confidence in our steps. Our colleague had relaxed us. Without minimizing the situation, he had helped us keep it in perspective.

3. *The third humor skill: a disciplined sense of joy in being alive.* No matter how difficult your life is, it is usually better than the alternative, and you can usually think of someone whose life is worse than yours. An individual we know recently learned that he has cancer. After hearing that his particular type of malignancy was treatable, he quickly shifted his focus from "Why me?" to "How do I make sure I am one of the survivors?" He talks about the cards he has been dealt as better than the ones others have been asked to play, including his own father who, at age 48, was left to raise nine small children by himself when his 46-year-old wife died. There are times when it is more difficult than others to find reasons for optimism and good cheer. Our friend has spread that unsinkable spirit around. His family is encouraged by his positive attitude, and his doctors are amazed at his physical progress because of it. He is proof that if we take the time and have the self-discipline, we can usually find a reason to smile and be glad we are alive.

The word *humor* comes from the Latin root *umor* which means moisture or fluidity. It was used originally to describe those body fluids responsible for a person's disposition, temperament, or mood. Too much of the wrong fluid produced melancholy. A good amount of the right fluid produced a balanced, flexible, healthy outlook on life, and the person who had it was often described as being able to maintain a sense of humor.

Experts who train people to use humor in business relationships say that it can be a valuable tool if it is used carefully. It is important to recognize the difference between humor that hurts and humor that helps. There is no need for humor at someone else's expense. Positive humor occurs between people who know each other and, according to C. W. Metcalf, "in one way or another, have gained each other's permission to use fun, laughter, play, or jokes to affirm their relationship."

Fred Gauss, an auditing supervisor, believes in lightening the workplace with positive humor.

> When I first started out, there were about 100 people working in the controller's office. We had a great camaraderie and there was a lot of humor in the office. One of the things we did, mostly because we had fairly regular turnover, was have roasts whenever someone got promoted or decided to leave our group for another opportunity. It started off simply, just a group of us going out to a local restaurant, but the roasts soon became an expected activity. I was one of the three designated emcees, and we got together and prepared jokes about each other and about the office. It was a healthy, fun outlet for us. A lot of the topics were about the politics going on back at the office. I did not feel this activity would hurt me with my bosses mostly because I had already shown I could do the work. We tried to keep things good-natured and fun. We poked fun at each other equally. Everyone had a chance to be singled out for some friendly ribbing.

Don't Forget

- Keep things in perspective. Be cordial, diplomatic, and cheerful even in difficult situations. Remember that the best way to gain power is by gaining the respect of others, and the best way to gain respect is to stay in control of yourself and your emotions.

On the other hand, negative humor is an attack disguised as a joke that allows the offender to avoid responsibility for his or her actions. Sarcasm is one of the most common forms of negative humor, and its effects can be devastating and demoralizing. Humor can be harmful when it is sarcastic, when it is used as a competitive weapon, or when it is used as a power play to exclude, embarrass, or offend someone else. Humor may be used to challenge or undermine authority and to make a point at someone else's expense.

Studies show that people who laugh and have fun are more productive, more creative, and more satisfied. One of our best consulting projects ever was with a manufacturing team that used humor to keep a critical new design project in perspective. Whenever the team met, one of the senior engineers would hang a cartoon on the door of the meeting room so that everyone had a smile on the way in. One cartoon showed a group of people rolling around the floor, holding their stomachs and laughing. The caption read: "You want this done by when?!" On another occasion, the team leader realized that discussion about the project had gone on for a long time and that the group had reached a temporary impasse. He had a special overhead transparency ready. It was a cartoon of a meeting room in which 10 puppies had their eyes closed and their heads down on the conference room table. The dog in front of the group was saying, "Would anyone else care to second the motion that we pause for an afternoon nap?"

There were many occasions when this project team used humor to ease tension. The team also went to lunch together whenever the members' schedules permitted, and they agreed not to work during this time. The social interaction was healthy and helpful. Team members got to know each other in a more personal way, and it helped them understand priorities and preferences when they got down to business again. Despite some difficult moments, the team completed the project on time and won a special company award for their efforts. The group decided that the best way to disband was at a celebration dinner where they remembered some of the best and worst moments of the project and then toasted each other's success on their new assignments. They ended their work together in a fun way.

When humor is positive and healthy, it can help individuals work together effectively and help each other through difficult times. But the wrong kind of humor can be harmful. Jokes that belittle or attack others can cause them to withdraw or look for ways to get even. Either reaction can damage teamwork and jeopardize our long-term work relationships.

This is the political side of humor, often described today by the words *politically correct*, in an effort to define what is fair, acceptable, and positive about our use of humor. In the right context, humor and the laughter it produces can improve camaraderie and reduce stress. An appropriate joke at the right time can relieve tension and help people let off steam. The right sense of humor can improve individual and team productivity, morale, and job satisfaction. Figure 10.1 highlights some of the important differences between positive and negative humor.

Danger!

- Before you start kidding around, know your audience. Be certain that you are not sending a message that you are minimizing or trivializing something that is important to them.

- Be extremely careful of humor that has a sexual nature. What may have been tolerated or accepted as appropriate years ago may be considered sexual harassment today.

Joseph Toto believes that wit can be contagious.

A sense of humor can convince others that you have perspective as well as wisdom. One of my best managers helped our whole team realize early in our work relationship that he was not out to get us, he was just doing what he needed to do. He was natural, gifted, and free-flowing. The result was that people liked him.

Research shows that humor can serve as a coping mechanism for people working closely together in both routine jobs or high-

POSITIVE HUMOR	versus	NEGATIVE HUMOR
Enhances communication		Damages communication
Enables learning		Blocks learning
Defuses anger		Causes anger
Promotes productivity		Hurts productivity
Optimistic		Pessimistic
Helps		Hurts
Affirms relationships		Destroys relationships
Builds camaraderie		Isolates and embarrasses others
Improves morale and teamwork		Fosters hostility and damages morale

Figure 10.1

pressure work environments. In 1957, Pamela Bradney studied department store personnel working in close quarters and showed that frequent joking allowed the staff "to avoid considerable tension and disagreement that would likely occur as a result of difficulties inherent in its formal structure." People are much more willing and able to try new approaches and develop new skills if they work in a comfortable environment.

Steve Ozer believes that a sense of humor is powerful.

It can help you diffuse tension and hostility if you use it well. It can help you humanize yourself and others. It builds bridges between people. It's a way to gain respect if it's not belittling or demeaning, if it's not at someone else's expense. It can make people feel comfortable with you. Helping people laugh at themselves can pave the way for a comfortable working relationship.

Being someone that people want to work with is important. Your manner, how personable you are, being someone whom others enjoy working with, getting results and having a comfortable working relationship with others—that's the challenge and probably the

Quick Tips

Q: Is a sense of humor conducive to a good work environment?

A: Research suggests that it helps in several ways. The ability to smile or laugh at yourself and the situations you encounter can help you keep an appropriate balance and perspective. Serious matters do not need to be so serious that they paralyze or incapacitate you. Usually there is some extenuating circumstance or alternative frame of reference that can mitigate even the most difficult problem. People with life-threatening diseases have gotten better by cultivating a healthy sense of humor. The same approach can help you in your work.

Q: Is there a negative side to humor?

A: Humor can be inappropriate and harmful when it is used to embarrass or exclude others. Laughing *at* someone can create bad feelings that are difficult to overcome. Laughing *with* someone means that you have established a comfortable relationship based on goodwill and good rapport. Humor can strengthen the connection and make it even more comfortable.

Q: What about people who use humor to offend others?

A: You cannot tolerate or accept humor that is sexist, racist, or discriminatory in any way. You have the responsibility to confront the person with pointed questions like, "Why do you think that is funny?" or "How would you feel if someone made a comment like that about you or your family?" Sometimes a hurtful joke is made out of ignorance or habit. That is no excuse. You must remind the person that their behavior is unacceptable to you.

core of effective office politics. Those people skills that make someone attractive in the sense that others are drawn to that person. Treating people with respect and listening, those softer skills make the difference. The *Wall Street Journal* had an article recently that described the importance of listening and how rare it is today to find someone who is really paying attention and not either talking or waiting to talk.

Don't Forget

- The reputation you develop over time is the most valuable thing you have. Office politics is a question of maintaining a reputation as a person who keeps things in perspective and does not get rattled by surprises.

Humor is also a way of relieving boredom among employees who are doing repetitive and routine tasks. Humor is often creative, playful, based on multiple meanings and interpretations that allow people to look at familiar situations in new and different ways. For example, the famous chocolate-wrapping, conveyor-belt scene from *I Love Lucy* makes us laugh out loud while at the same time we realize the dangers of misrepresenting our job performance. By stuffing candy into their blouses and hats or eating whatever extra pieces they cannot wrap quickly enough, Lucy and Ethel appear to be keeping up with the pace of their jobs. Their reward for this apparent, but false, success is completely unexpected: their supervisor says "Speed it up!" and the conveyor belt sends new challenges and more chocolates their way.

Humor is a very powerful way of opening people up to new ideas and showing a new twist to old notions. In the movie, *Young Frankenstein,* for example, the title character demonstrates the importance of clear communication when he sends his assistant to find a brain for the monster he has created. Instead of finding the perfect replacement, Igor settles for the brain of someone he says was labeled "A.B. Normal." We have all learned lessons about communication from Abbott and Costello's hilarious routine, "Who's on First?" We have gained humorous insights about routine compassion, patience, and persistence from classic performances by Charley Chaplin or Laurel and Hardy. Cartoon characters like Bugs Bunny and Wile E. Coyote have made us laugh at our own human foibles, and whether it is *Seinfeld, Laugh In,* or *Saturday Night Live,* television has provided a steady menu of funny perspectives on our work life situations.

Lila Green believes that humor in the work setting is especially important for women.

> Many women are afraid to use humor on the job because they are concerned that they may not appear businesslike or serious. This may be a mistake. Both men and women can take their work seriously and take themselves lightly. Appropriate, timely, and tasteful humor is always a benefit. I hope the sound that will shatter the glass ceiling will be the sound of laughter.

For Aleene Maiaroto, mortgage loan officer, maintaining a positive attitude is extremely important.

> I can't do my job unless I have other people on my side. So I do things to help lighten the mood and that helps me be well-liked and respected. Nasty or mean doesn't work. We work in a very stressful environment—people's lives depend on our decisions about their mortgages—people call us in tears, and they are worried about their tight settlement timetables. Tension runs high, and people depend on me to be in a good mood—to tell a joke, to tell them they're doing a good job, to go to lunch with them, to take them to lunch, or just to spread some "Aleene cheer" around the office. It doesn't take a lot to be pleasant and to help change the mood in our office.

We know an executive named Doug who assembled all of the managers and supervisors who reported to him for an important strategic planning meeting. He carefully prepared a binder of material for each participant complete with graphs, spreadsheets, budgeting projections, and a small stack of other status reports. Realizing how heavy the information was, Doug decided to lighten things up with a humorous front-page cartoon he had found in one of Gary Larsen's *Far Side* books. In the picture, there is a house and a gated front yard. There is a young boy with big glasses peering around a large tree near the house. He has a menacing smile on his face. Hanging on the gate is a warning sign: "Beware of Doug." When participants at the meeting opened their binders and saw the cartoon, there was a round of hearty laughter, and Doug welcomed them warmly.

For Katherine Huston, a sense of humor has often eased tension and set a tone for difficult meetings.

I was recently conducting a training program on pay-for-performance goal setting. The managers in my class were resisting the idea of having to tell people how they were really doing on their jobs. I finally said, "I'm not here because I am an expert on goal set-ting or an expert on performance management. I am here because I am a senior-level black-belt Akido Master, and I understand *that's* what it's going to take to get this group to try this new management process." With that, I had them in the palm of my hand.

Don't Forget

- Humor is personal and individual. What makes you laugh may not be funny to someone else. Age, background, culture, lifestyle, and other factors determine the jokes we tell or retell because they have already made us smile.

Companies are proving that humor has the ability to improve productivity, develop teamwork, boost morale, and reduce job turnover. When people enjoy where they work, they are more likely to contribute and stay. A recent survey conducted by Accountemps showed that 96 percent of those executives surveyed believe that people with a sense of humor do better at their jobs than those who have little or no sense of humor.

Humor consultant, C. W. Metcalf, offers seminars and training sessions to companies throughout the world in which he encourages participants in the following areas.

- Overcome terminal professionalism and stop taking yourself too seriously.

- Take yourself lightly and your job seriously.
- Understand that you are not the center of the universe.
- Do something for the fun of it.
- Expect the best.

According to Metcalf, what makes it possible for people to stop and laugh at difficult problems is their ability to find something outrageous or incongruous: "The trick in these situations is to find absurdity in the adversity." It is the ability we all have to look back and laugh at awkward moments, once we have gotten over our initial embarrassment. Some of our funniest memories today are based on difficult and sometimes even painful events that time has helped us look at now in a different way. Like watching our personal version of *America's Funniest Home Videos,* we are able to laugh at a painful slip on the ice, smile at an embarrassing sports accident, or grin with others at a mistake that any of us could have made. It is this ability to find a common ground even in our worst misfortunes that makes humor a beneficial healing process for us all.

Shortcut

- Try using a sense of humor when you have to deliver a difficult or uncomfortable message. Try to come up with an approach that is easier for the recipient to accept and understand. We know a manager who recently had to begin discussing her company's downsizing plan with her staff. One person was out sick that day, so the manager started her meeting by saying, "Let me assure you that Mary has a cold and will probably be back at work on Thursday. Contrary to the rumors some of us have been hearing or even spreading, she has not resigned, retired, or found a new job. Like it or not, therefore, we still need to talk about our current work functions and the number of people we can justify to do those jobs." This introduction drew a few smiles and at least eased the tension. Sometimes a direct statement may seem too serious or too sensitive. A lighter, more relaxed approach can often get better results.

Humorous training programs like those offered by Video Arts have become popular in recent years because they're so effective. As John Cleese, the British comedian and founder of Video Arts, explains, "The advantage of comedy is that it affects trainees at a level that isn't entirely conscious. In fact, I think the main evolutionary significance of our sense of humor is that it gets us from the closed mode to the open mode quicker than anything else." For example, in the company's video, *Straight Talking: The Art of Assertiveness,* the announcer begins the program by explaining: "The title of this program is assertiveness. We were going to call it a program that sort of deals with ways of slightly improving your chances of kind of getting what you want from other people just a tiny bit if that's all right with you. But we felt that it was: a) not very catchy; and b) not very assertive."

The ability of humor to relax people and ease stress also makes it an ideal, low-tech productivity booster that can improve employees' mental health and reduce sick time.

The idea that humor can improve productivity is also supported by Howard Pollio, professor of psychology at the University of Tennessee at Knoxville. In a study measuring the effect of humor on the ability to accomplish routine production tasks, he discovered groups that are performing repetitive tasks do better when they're having fun. In a *Personnel Journal* article (June, 1992) he says, "Humor can alleviate boredom and buoy everyone up. Humor doesn't detract from more complicated group problem-solving activities, even though the ability of humor to engage and enliven people is sometimes counterbalanced by its distracting qualities. Still, the notion that laughter interferes with group performance is a myth."

Ironically, humor in organizations is often serious communication. It has a purpose, a methodology, and a value that can provide important insights about the nature of social interactions between individuals and work groups. The funny outer layers may hide a deeper, more important message. The ability to laugh at yourself can help others feel more comfortable with you, can help you be willing to keep your mistakes in perspective, and can help you cope with stressful work pressures.

✔ When you are feeling unusual pressure or stress, try to walk away from the situation long enough to regain a positive perspective or a more optimistic point of view. Ask yourself questions like: "How important is this activity to my life and my career?" or "What will people say about this a year from now?"

✔ Use humor that is positive and not sarcastic or hurtful. Although humor is personal and individual, there is usually some common ground that will make most people laugh or at least smile. Focusing on a humorous point of view that others share can help you establish and maintain a comfortable working relationship with them.

✔ Humor is conducive to a successful work environment. Without minimizing the seriousness of certain important activities, you can help others keep an appropriate perspective so that problems or crises do not paralyze you or undermine your efforts.

◆▬◆◆◆◆◆◆◆◆◆◆◆◆◆◆◆◆◆◆◆◆◆◆◆◆◆◆◆◆◆

CHAPTER 11

The Negative Impact of Dirty Politics

◆◆◆◆◆◆◆◆◆◆◆◆◆◆◆◆◆◆◆◆◆◆◆◆◆◆◆◆◆◆◆

The person who practices devious political tactics does so at considerable career risk. Practicing unsavory office politics may lead you to being unwanted, unloved, and fired. In extreme cases, you might even be sued for libel or punched in the face.—**Andrew DuBrin,** *Winning Office Politics* **(Prentice Hall, 1990)**

Negative politics is created when I feel the organization in some way owns me and leads me to believe that moving ahead in the organization is good for me and helpful to my self-esteem. If my primary vehicle for feeling empowered is to move up the ladder in a system that offers little autonomy, I am forced to operate in manipulative ways.—**Peter Block,** *The Empowered Manager* **(Jossey-Bass, 1988)**

Having grown up in traditional, hierarchical companies with patriarchal values and tightly structured organizational charts, too many people believe, according to Peter Block, that in order to manage the politics of their situation, they must become good at:

• Manipulating situations and, at times, other people
• Managing or controlling information to their own advantage

◆◆

- Using the names of high-level people when seeking support for their pet projects

- Managing relationships in calculating and self-protective ways

- Believing that, in order to get ahead, they must be cautious in telling the truth and circumspect in the way they deliver any message that might seem contrary to what key people in the company want to hear

These negative political techniques have been reinforced, of course, by countless horror stories about people who have been fired, reassigned to entry-level positions, or ignored for new projects because they dared to "tell it like it is," they dared to tell the truth. Unfortunately, "they kill messengers" has become a popular excuse for ignoring organizational realities. Those who play these games believe it is more important for you to look healthy and keep your best face on. Do not let anyone know when something's gone wrong, even if you have to withhold potentially harmful information, bend the truth to pacify your boss, or even lie to keep your job.

An employee for one of our clients recently said, "I cannot possibly confront that situation and tell my boss what I really think about the decision he made." When we asked, "When was the last time anyone around here got fired for challenging a manager's opinion?," the thoughtful employee had to admit, "Even if it has never happened, it could—and I just cannot take the chance that I'll be the first." That fear is not uncommon in today's work world where downsizing, reengineering, and other efforts to streamline operations are often viewed as euphemisms for getting fired by people who are most affected or endangered. The safer alternative is to engage in questionable political activities that buy people time and convince them, at least temporarily, that they are just playing the game like everyone else.

Actually, to survive in what appears to be a hostile environment, many people resort to selfish and manipulative behaviors. Sometimes it becomes difficult for them to change their perspective about what is really going on and how their negative actions are only making matters worse. It is often too easy to fall into a vicious cycle in which playing dirty seems to be acknowledged, rewarded, and encouraged as an acceptable way of doing business.

If you are tempted to try negative politics as a temporary strategy or as a permanent way of life, remember that there are potentially significant downsides to these self-serving practices. Most organizations today opt for teamwork and collaboration instead of the compulsive freewheeling competitive style Michael Maccoby described in his 1976 bestseller, *The Gamesman.*

> The modern gamesman is best defined as a person who loves change and wants to influence its course. He likes to take calculated risks and is fascinated by techniques and new methods. He sees a developing project, human relations, and his own career in terms of options and possibilities, as if they were a game.
>
> He is energized to compete not because he wants to build an empire, not for riches, but rather for fame, glory, the exhilaration of gaining victories. His main goal is to be known as a winner, and his deepest fear is to be labeled as a loser.

To make sure that you are not guilty of dirty politics or manipulative behavior, here are a few activities you need to avoid.

1. Do not badmouth others in public, whether or not they have earned your negative criticism.

An alternative: Praise in public, criticize in private. Go directly to the person causing you concerns and work hard to resolve any differences of opinions or conflicts. If that effort does not succeed, enlist the help of someone else, probably your mutual supervisor, to correct the situation. Involving as few people as possible is the best approach. Others may be embarrassed to hear you airing out your disagreement with a coworker or your work team's dirty linen in public. Also, if your associates hear you publicly criticizing another peer, they may conclude that you would likely do the same about them if you ever had a reason to do so. This will surely create an atmosphere of suspicion in which others will be careful about what they say and how they act when you are around.

2. Do not take credit for someone else's work or let another person take responsibility for one of your mistakes.

An alternative: Fair is fair when it comes to your own job performance. Allowing others to have an exaggerated assessment of your accomplishments will only set you up for failure and set them up for future disappointment. Succeeding on someone else's merits can put you in the untenable position of having to produce results far beyond your current level of competence. Better to share the credit or give it back to those who have earned it. There will be less pressure on you to extend yourself beyond your capabilities. Honesty is also best when it comes to problems that others are willing to minimize, blame themselves for, or overlook. For example, you may have an excellent performance track record that creates what experts have called a *halo effect* when a real problem occurs. Your supervisor or coworkers may excuse or dismiss the current problem simply because it is so rare for something like this to happen to you. Be grateful that your reputation softens this event, but do not miss an opportunity to learn from your mistakes and improve your performance. Conversely, if you are the victim of a "horned effect" (because of previous problems, others do not give you adequate credit for a recent success), be prepared to set the record straight and seek the recognition you deserve.

3. Do not be a cynic or a chronic complainer.

An alternative: Maintain a positive outlook about your job, your profession, and your company. If you cannot be upbeat and manage your own morale in your current position, start taking immediate steps to change your situation. Letting others know you are dissatisfied and blaming others for your unfortunate predicament will wear thin on even your staunchest allies. Most people are quickly demoralized by venting coworkers, and your critical comments will be perceived as a counterproductive waste of their valuable time.

Do what you can to make things better. If that does not work or help you feel more optimistic, admit to yourself that it is time for you to try something else. Then take steps to make a change.

4. Do not ignore established protocols for resolving problems or initiating new ideas.

An alternative: Be certain you understand how things are done in your company. For example, is it ever acceptable to bypass your supervisor when you need approval or support for one of your favorite projects? If you have a recurring problem with your boss, where do you go for help? If you hear complaints about a coworker or another department, how do you get things resolved satisfactorily? Before you take action in any of these potentially awkward, inflammatory situations, it always pays to know how similar problems have been dealt with in the past. Understanding precedence and priorities will help you stay politically correct.

5. Challenging established traditions or questioning commonly held company values.

An alternative: Know when it is safe to disagree with senior managers and veteran employees. Many of the people you work with may take a great deal of pride in having helped your company achieve its current reputation or level of success. They may be proud of positions, policies, and procedures that you view as outdated or obsolete. Take care that you are not too cavalier in your treatment of what others may consider sacred beliefs or special rituals. Change is often useful or necessary. But, whenever you are recommending something new, be sensitive to those individuals who built and staked their reputations on "the way things have always been done around here." Highlight the positive benefits of a new approach without making the old way seem foolish or ill-conceived.

Sometimes you may find that you are on the receiving end of another person's unscrupulous or malicious behavior. When you need to confront someone else who is playing dirty politics, know that dealing with manipulators, back-stabbers, and other dirty politicians requires careful strategy and skillful self-preservation techniques. The most important thing to remember is that you must confront, and not avoid, the situation. Here are some ways to gain the advantage or maintain your ground.

1. Gather your facts so that you are prepared to describe when particular incidents have occurred and how they have had a negative impact on you or your work team's performance. Collect specific data about increased costs, missed deadlines, lost productivity, decreased morale, and any other quantifiable side effects of this person's behavior.

2. Indicate your concern about these issues and give the other person the benefit of the doubt by stating you are certain he or she is also concerned about the causes and effects of this problem. Emphasize that your purpose in confronting the situation is to work together to find a mutually satisfactory resolution.

3. Insist that you and the other person play by universally accepted, well-established rules. List the key points that are not negotiable in this conversation. For example, "No name-calling," or "Let's agree to stick to the facts and keep assumptions out of this discussion," or "If we reach a stalemate or an impasse, we will ask a neutral third party to help us." Ask the other person to discuss any ground rules he or she would like to add, then agree to stick to the rules you have established. If you cannot agree at this point, let the other person know your only recourse is to get help from your supervisor or some other impartial resource.

4. Ask open-ended questions to get a thorough understanding of the other person's views about past incidents and future practices. Get the individual to answer questions like: "Why do you think that approach is better than the one others have tried successfully?" or "How do you think I should respond to your public insults?" or "How would you react if the situation were reversed, and I was spreading negative rumors about you?" The purpose at this point is to try to understand what you have done

to incite this person's dirty approach and to determine the best way to stop it.

5. Hold your ground and do not yield to threats or other attempts to manipulate you into an uncomfortable position. Be firm and persistent, even if it takes every ounce of energy and courage. The negative politician must understand that fair play is the only way you are willing to play the game.

6. Document your perception of the situation so that you have valid data to support your side of the issue. If the behavior is not corrected, minimize the amount of contact you have with that person. If it is impossible to avoid contact, ask a trustworthy advocate or sponsor to help you manage the relationship and perhaps even be with you whenever you need to interact with this difficult person.

One of the people we interviewed gave this perspective on dirty politics.

> Dirty politicians succeed early on but not for long. They take good people down with them. They are often too careless, too ruthless, and they develop as many enemies as allies. Unfortunately, there's still a skew in our society that believes someone who is sharp and incisive is better then someone who is kind. There is still a belief that this brash and abrasive type of person is a little brighter, a little more intelligent. What they actually may be is just a little nastier. That behavior is sometimes rewarded early on, because these people look like bright, aggressive go-getters when, in fact, they may just be mean. When people catch on to this pattern of behavior, dirty politicians often discover that they have alienated those who might have helped them.

When you deal with a dirty politician, therefore, try using some of these techniques.

- Stay on their good side instead of dodging their bullets. Do not get drawn into their petty turf wars.

- Keep a record of your interactions with them. Document which ideas are yours, which aren't, and who needs to know the score.

NEGATIVE POLITICS
Manipulative
Win-Lose
Aggressive
Tries to Outdo
Emphasizes Self-Interests
Takes a Narrow View (Snapshot)
Focuses on Short-Term Measures
Power Hungry
Creates Resentment
Artificial
Destructive
Contrived and False
Emphasizes Taking and Withholding
Thrives on Flattery

Figure 11.1

Remember, dirty politicians often steal or take credit for someone else's good work.

- Send someone else you trust duplicates of memos and e-mail you send to these dirty politicians.

- Do not play their game. If possible, avoid spending time with them. If unavoidable, minimize your time alone with them. Try instead to have a buffer with you, preferably an objective witness, to guard against any negative outcomes.

Negative politics can damage relationships, dampen morale, and destroy productivity. Figure 11.1 highlights some of the problems associated with negative politics. Manipulation, for example, is one of the highest forms of selfishness and disrespect. The message being sent is "Let me tell you what's best for you—which also happens to be exactly what's best for me." Do a careful assessment of the way you accomplish things at work. If you determine that you always win, that you always get exactly what you want, or that you always have the last word, take a closer look at your political motives and activities. You may, in fact, be guilty (inadvertently or not) of dirty politics and manipulative behavior. The cost to you in credibility, trust, respect, and future successes may be more than you are willing to pay. The choice, therefore, may be a simple one: change!

CHAPTER 12

◆◆◆◆◆◆◆◆◆◆◆◆◆◆◆◆◆◆◆◆◆◆◆◆◆◆◆◆◆◆◆◆◆◆◆◆◆

The Benefits of Fair Play

◆◆◆◆◆◆◆◆◆◆◆◆◆◆◆◆◆◆◆◆◆◆◆◆◆◆◆◆◆◆◆◆◆◆◆◆◆

Work is the search for daily meaning and daily bread.—**Studs Terkel,** *Working*

If you treat people right, they will treat you right 90 percent of the time.—**Franklin D. Roosevelt**

Fair play is a matter of intelligence not emotions. It always helps to understand the rules of the game, the positions that others are going to play, the strategies they may use against you, and the options you have available. Having choices gives you control over your life and your work. Knowing you have options keeps you from falling into ruts or routines that can make you feel powerless and defeated.

Sometimes people succumb to comfortable habits, they simply fall into step and continue doing what they have always done without thinking about their actions or measuring their progress. When they finally get jolted into realizing what has been going on, they may become angry or bitter about what others have done to hold them back or keep them in place. It is one thing to be a victim when someone else is not playing fair; it is quite another thing to blame another for a situation you yourself have created or contributed to.

◆◆◆

Reflection is one of the best ways to keep yourself from being lulled into a potentially dangerous situation. Take a rational, logical approach and start by analyzing your current situation. A little introspection can give you important insights about where you are, where you want to go, who or what is standing in the way, and how you will know when you have arrived at your next target destination. This information is the basis, then, for you to determine how to play the game fairly.

Then, if you play the game well and lose, be a good loser. It can help strengthen your position for the next competition. Sore losers have a way of bringing out the worst in all of us. We react to them more aggressively and less rationally. However, good losers evoke feelings of respect and accomplishment. On the other hand, we also admire good winners, people who let us walk away with our own self-esteem intact. We may even look forward to our next interaction with someone who has challenged our skills and not attacked our values or our personality. We all have met worthy adversaries at chess, Scrabble, basketball, meeting sales quotas, winning safety contests, and other competitive activities. What makes them worthy is they play by the rules and do not violate our right to walk away with our heads up after the most intense interaction. We boo the cheap shots and applaud the magnanimous victors who shake our hands in recognition of our efforts.

Here's a checklist to help make sure that you play fair when you are in healthy competition with someone else.

1. *Make certain you know what you want and why.* It is important to have both a long-range plan and a series of short-term goals and deadlines that will help you move along in the right direction. For some, a road map analogy can help: mark the spot that is your next destination, determine how long it will take for you to get there and how much you can afford to spend to get where you want to be, decide if there are any attractions along the way that would make the journey more enjoyable, anticipate any disruptive detours you need to avoid, and start your trip with a useful planning tool

that you can check on regularly to make sure you are on the road to success. Another important part of this activity is defining what is negotiable or nonnegotiable for you. The negotiables are those areas where you are willing to bend, give in a little, cut corners, let another person have his or her way, lose a little ground now for a greater gain later, or simply not go to the mat because the issue is not important enough to waste your time, money, or energy on it. Your nonnegotiables, however, are limits imposed on you by law or adopted by you because of your personal, moral, or ethical values. It is important to reflect on these principles occasionally and to make certain they remain part of your automatic, authentic response to work situations. We have met many talented business-people who live by a personal code of ethics that includes nonnegotiables like telling the truth, treating others with compassion and dignity, giving others credit for their accomplishments, and respecting diversity and individual differences.

2. *State clearly your objectives and desired outcomes.* Make sure that others know what you are trying to accomplish, why your objectives are important, how you plan to achieve them, and how they can contribute to your desired outcomes or collaborate with you to meet or exceed expectations. If these conversations are conducted in a spirit of mutual trust and respect, you and others will be able to resolve any potentially harmful conflict and arrive at options that will help everyone move forward successfully. Letting others who affect your goals or who are affected by them know exactly how your work involves them can establish a relationship where teamwork becomes more important than competition.

3. *Stay calm and focused on your ultimate goal.* The old adage, Rome was not built in a day, can be an important reminder as you move forward toward your ultimate goal. Try not to be discouraged by obstacles, detours, or temporary setbacks. Remember that you are in charge of your own destiny and your own morale. Whenever you meet with resistance or someone else seems to be playing dirty, take a step back, reassess the situation, and maintain your self-

confidence and your commitment to your own nonnegotiables. Be patient and persistent in your steady, determined approach to your ultimate objective.

4. *Be thoughtful, analytical, and rational in your approach so that your emotions don't get in the way or out of control.*   Ask yourself questions about the situation (not the people involved) and its impact on your work (not you personally). You may be getting angry or frustrated by what's going on, but the most important question is "Why?" An objective, data-based response can often help you determine your deeper, work-related concerns such as: you are missing deadlines, going over budget, causing backlogs for other departments, not providing quality service to your customers, taking work home with you more often than usual, causing unnecessary waste, increasing your work group's error rate, or any number of other work-specific problems that make this particular situation important enough to confront and resolve. Remember that some detours are unavoidable. But ones that take you too far off track need to be addressed and remedied as soon as possible.

5. *Take your time and be willing to go with the flow as long as it is moving you in the right direction.*   Try not to sweat the small stuff. Even your most carefully conceived plans will rarely go exactly the way you thought they would. There will always be surprises—some pleasant, some painful. Learn to take the occasional bumps in stride. Some potholes are bigger and more damaging than others. But if you stay alert and keep your eye on the road ahead, you will learn to anticipate and ultimately avoid some of the usual, most annoying obstacles. Learn to slow down when caution is required; learn to speed up when it is safe, reasonable, or necessary to do so. Whatever you decide to do, make sure that you stay in control.

6. *Learn from your mistakes so that they help and not hurt you along the way.*   Remember that even the most successful gold prospectors had to sift through a lot of sand before they found the occasional golden nugget. Sometimes trial and error is the only way

we have to find the hidden pearl or the sunken treasure. George Bernard Shaw once said that, "A life making mistakes is not only more honorable but more useful than a life spent doing nothing." Mistakes are inevitable. The key to eventual success is to make mistakes useful, to learn from them and move on. When you make a mistake, admit it and then try to understand why it happened and how it can help you do things better the next time. Do not minimize or rationalize a mistake, and try not to let others write it off before you have carefully analyzed the causes and effects of the mistake. Do not offer excuses, point your finger, or assign blame to others, even if they were part of the problem. Take responsibility for your actions, focus on what you can do to improve, and use the experience as a learning opportunity. Offer a solution, "I will call the customer and discuss the problem with her," or a future alternative, "From now on, I will double-check our available inventory before placing an order with our supplier." Do not dwell on your mistake, but make sure that others know that you are taking steps to resolve the problem and that this will not happen again.

7. *Work with what you know and try not to worry about the unknown.* Along with the fear of failure, fear of the unknown is one of our most common fears. It can be paralyzing and counterproductive. Many people resist any type of change at all because they would rather accept the familiar (even if their current situation is boring, depressing, or painful) than take a chance on something new or different. Have you ever been in a situation where you catastrophized about an upcoming event, like a visit to your dentist or a sales presentation, and then discovered that your worst fears were far greater than what actually happened? Have you ever heard yourself or others say, "Well, that wasn't as bad as I thought it would be?" or "If I had known then how easy this would be, I would have done it long ago?" If you allow yourself too much time to worry about the unknown, you will probably come up with countless reasons to maintain the status quo, stay where you are, and waste valuable time and energy getting yourself ready to deal with imaginary

disappointments. Instead of dwelling on what could go wrong, take a direct and timely assessment of what you know. Focus on: Why are you moving in this direction? What are the potential benefits to you and others? What could go wrong? Have things like this ever gone wrong for you in the past and if so, how often? What is the worst thing that could happen and what would you do if it did? This type of contingency plan can help you understand, anticipate, and address potential problems. Rather than giving you reasons to stay where you are, this quick analysis can actually help you proceed with confidence.

8. *Listen to your hunches, those insights that surprise you when you least expect them.*   Creative thinking requires curiosity, openness, and a willingness to search for new ways to look at familiar things. Creativity expert Edward de Bono describes the process as looking for the "po"—the potential, the poetry, the possibilities of a situation—instead of the "no." Many people have learned not to trust their hunches and to ignore the intuitive process in favor of something that is more logical and acceptable. Instead of playing around with the "what if's," they concentrate on all the reasons why a new idea will not or cannot work. Brainstorming for a variety of possible options becomes less important than finding the right answer or the only way to proceed. Being logical and practical is often the best approach. But there are times when an off-the-wall idea can lead you in an exciting new direction. There has been a lot of research about how the two sides of our brains respond to problems in different ways. The right side is more ambiguous, conceptual, speculative and innovative. The left side is logical, analytical, critical, and concrete. Both types of thinking play an important part in any problem-solving process, but most people have a preferred way of processing information.

Right-brain people process information from whole to part. They usually see the big picture easily but struggle with the details. Left-brain people process information from part to whole. They prefer a step-by-step logical sequence of events but may have difficulty visualizing the big picture.

When you are confronting an issue, right-brain thinking can help you search for new ideas, generate a variety of choices, take a broader perspective, and look at the problem in different ways. Left-brain thinking can then help you evaluate the ideas, narrow your choices, analyze contingencies or risks, and prepare a strategy to implement the solution you ultimately select. It is important to trust your intuitive side and not rush too quickly to find the best, the right, the most practical, or the only answer. An occasional surprise insight can be good for you.

Whenever you are in healthy competition with someone who is also playing fair, enjoy the interaction the way you would enjoy a good chess game or a good tennis match, not as a battle to be won or lost but as a challenge to be resolved satisfactorily. Remember that office politics is an inevitable aspect of your daily work life. You cannot avoid these types of interactions, and you should not minimize their importance to you or to others. As Joel DeLuca reminds us in *Political Savvy* (LRP Publications, 1992):

> Many individuals are not very active when it comes to organizational politics. They *respond* to events as they occur but generally keep their heads down and avoid getting involved. Others sit back with their eyes open to the political scene and try to *predict* what might happen so they can be prepared ahead of time. A few go much further and *initiate* strong action in the political arena. Although the actual degree of activity varies from situation to situation, people often express clear preferences in terms of how active they want to become.

You have choices about how often you get involved and how well you are willing to play the game. Figure 12.1 highlights some of the benefits of positive politics.

The appropriate use of office politics makes it possible for you to negotiate priorities, arrange for resources, collaborate on complex projects, and achieve outstanding results in an environment built on effective communication and productive interactions. Ideally, office politics can help you and your organization thrive in a spirit of

POSITIVE POLITICS
Straightforward
Win-Win
Collaborative
Builds
Emphasizes Greater Good
Takes Panoramic View
A Long-Term Strategy
Empowering
Creates Credibility
Genuine
Productive
Honest and Fair
Emphasizes Sharing
Welcomes Recognition

Figure 12.1

cooperation, trust, and mutual respect. Working for a greater good can often inspire the collaborative approach we have advocated throughout this book and make it the practical reality for you that it has already become in many of today's most successful organizations.

From a personal perspective, if you master these positive political skills, you will be able to manage and monitor your own performance and job satisfaction. You will have a clear conscience and sleep better at night. You will not need to waste your time looking over your shoulder or wondering who is about to retaliate for one of your negative attacks. You will be more optimistic about your future, more in control of your own destiny, more certain that you deserve credit for your accomplishments, and more comfortable with your role as a contributing team player. You will have work relationships built on credibility, trust, and mutual respect. You will enjoy a reputation for ethical and responsible behavior.

Office politics, therefore, is not something to avoid or misuse. It is something to embrace and pursue conscientiously, skillfully, and ethically. It can make a difference for you today and in all of your future work efforts.

Index

About the Authors

William A. Salmon is an independent management consultant and writer specializing in organizational behavior. Formerly Senior Vice President at W.K. Gray & Associates, a major management and organizational development firm, he has spent the past 15 years providing consulting services to a wide range of clients including CIGNA Corporation, Johnson & Johnson, and Kraft Dairy Group.

Rosemary T. Salmon is a partner in Salmon & Salmon Associates, a management consulting company she helped launch in 1989. In addition to managing the company's computer and information technology, she has had exclusive design and editorial responsibility for all the company's writing and training projects. Prior to this, Rosemary was head nurse in several general hospitals, at a geriatric center, and in Active Admissions at a psychiatric facility.